The Life and Times of
Acharya Mahaprajna

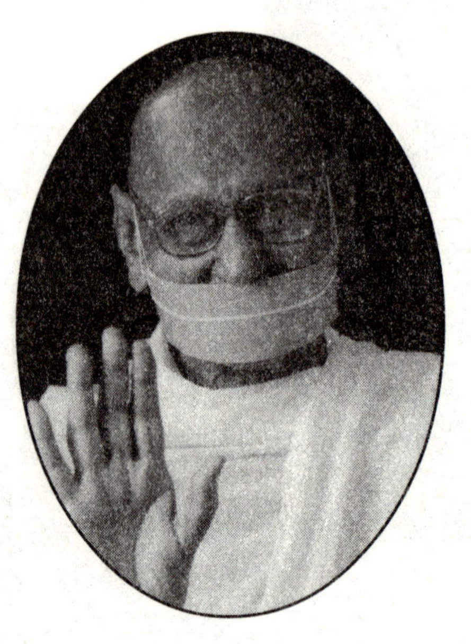

The Life and Times of
Acharya Mahaprajna

U.S. Durga

Published by
Ocean Books (P) Ltd.
4/19 Asaf Ali Road,
New Delhi-110 002 (INDIA)
e-mail: info@oceanbooks.in

ISBN 978-81-8430-231-8
The Life and Times of
ACHARYA MAHAPRAJNA
by U.S. Durga

Edition
2025

Price
₹ 300.00 (Rupees Three Hundred only)

Printed at
Print Media, New Delhi

Dedication

I wanted to present the book as a birthday gift to revered Acharya Mahaprajna, on his completion of ninety years of age, but everything is determined by forces over which we have no control. I am happy that he had a look at the manuscript and gave me his blessings for my first attempt in writing. I know that the small step cannot enumerate all the virtues of the great personality but I have made efforts to understand him and his religion.

Contents

JAINISM

for Better Health and Wellness

I

DELHI had been announced as the new capital of British India; New Delhi, the modern part of Delhi was fast coming up to house the residence of the Viceroy. At the beck and call of this great Viceroy and on his whims and fancies 500 and odd petty kings of native states managed the vast Indian sub-continent. About 200 kilometres southwest of Delhi at 5.40 pm on 14th June 1920 in the Thar desert in the village of Tamkor, dominated by mud huts, in the native Jaipur state, a male child was born to Balubai and Tolaram.

Merciful and pathetic cries of the people of the Jalianwala Bagh massacre at Amritsar on 13th April 1919 were still on the minds of their countrymen. In the season of the burning sun and dust storms, the desert winds gathered the sand into long whirling columns, rising high starting from the mounds and moving skywards carrying with them bits and pieces of dried leaves, straws and twigs. To the villagers these storms were like large monsters swirling, howling and blowing off the fragile, thatched roofs of the poor villagers' huts in the desert. To the ordinary mortals such settings hardly foretold the birth of a great saintly soul, of the preacher of peace and universal brotherhood on Mother Earth.

It was a rather hot and sultry summer afternoon, the sun overhead and the baked ground underfoot were merciless. Balubai was busy working in the backyard of the house. Balubai, suddenly, had a vibration in her body and before she could realize, the baby was expelled out of her abdomen. Jadaavbai, Tolaram's sister, who was keeping an eye on her sister-in-law's movements, looked outside and rushed towards Balubai anxiously.

She saw that it was a baby boy and laughed with joy. He was bawling. He was as fair as his father. According to the forefathers, a boy presaged the special blessings of God not only upon the parents but also upon the parents' families; and there was the proud knowledge that the name of Tolaram would thus be both distinguished and perpetuated.

The child's umbilical cord was cut with the knife, kept especially for the purpose, in a high recess and used over and over again for the children born in the family; and the child was cleaned in soothing warm water, heated in an earthen pot by burning dry sticks and cow dungcakes in the earthen floor's shallow fire hole. She whispered the prayer to the five universal supreme beings, which throws light on the qualities of the revered ones, in the ear of the newborn,

Obeisance to the Victors (*Arhats*).
Obeisance to the Liberated Souls (*Sidhas*).
Obeisance to the preceptors (*Acharyas*).
Obeisance to the Spiritual Teachers (*Upadhyayas*).
Obeisance to all the Saints (*Sadhus*) in the world.

(This sublime five-fold obeisance destroys all the sins and is supremely auspicious.)

Both mother and the child were shifted to a windowless bedroom of the old-fashioned house, hurriedly turned into a labour room and the room was lit by an earthen lamp 24 hours a day. A curtain was hung on the door of the room.

It was a moment of pride in the life of Jadaavbai. Her parents had died. She was playing the role of her mother in the welcome rituals and caress, and in nursing the baby and post-delivery care of her sister-in-law. Jadaavbai performed witchcraft to ward off the evil spirits away from the infant. Then, she produced the lusty sound of beating on the back of a *thali* (large bell metal eating plate) with a *belan* (a wooden rolling pin) starting from near the ear of the newborn to all the nooks and corners of the house and ended on the top of the house. It was an announcement of the birth of a baby boy in the village. Congratulating her, all the members of the family echoed the omens of good fortune.

Jadaavbai asked her elder brother to perform the ritual of giving the first feeding to the child. He put a few drops of honey in the mouth of the child by squeezing cotton soaked in honey. It is a common belief that a child would develop seven of the characteristics of the person whoever gives him first feed. He went to consult *Panditji,* the family Hindu priest, for ceremonial rituals to fix a date for the naming ceremony.

A telegram was sent to Tolaram at Phoolwari, 1500 miles away in East Bengal now Bangladesh, where he was running his business. A message was sent to Balubai's father Hiralal, at Khinwasar telling of the birth of the child and date of his naming ceremony.

The message of the birth of a grandchild thrilled Dhapubai, Balubai's mother, who was waiting for the news and started arranging new clothes for Balubai and clothes, a gold chain, a ring and *Nath*—rings for ears and nose—for her newborn and many more things for the ceremony. Tikamchand, Balubai's brother, ordered the camel cart to be ready so that he could reach Tamkor to attend the naming ceremony.

Tamkor was a tiny village with a few grocery and sweet shops opening on a wide courtyard for vendors, who visited the village on camels. It had only a few stone and lime mortar *havelis,* built mostly by merchant families, amidst a cluster of thatched roof huts with low walled courtyards facing narrow lanes and radiating outward from the centre. Soon the lanes dwindled into footpaths and got lost in the surrounding sand dunes.

One of *havelis'* was the home of Seth Binjraj. Binjraj had four sons, Gopichand, Balchand, Tolaram and Pannalal and each son had a quarter of it to live there with his family as he liked. They were Bisa Oswals. Their forefathers say that they belong to *Rajputs,* a clan reputed to place great value on etiquette and military virtues.

They accepted the path of non-violence and vegetarianism of Mahavira and are adherents of his philosophy and called Jains, eschewing any occupation, which even remotely endangers animal life, and are engaged largely in commerce and finance. The villagers called them by their profession, *Banias* (merchants). *Banias* also comprised of followers of Hindu religion. The two cultures were miraculously flowing side by side without a dent in brotherhood.

On the morning of the naming ceremony the community barber went around the village inviting all the Jain families to bless the newborn. The child and his mother were given a bath in the labour room by the barber's wife Dhapa, in water boiled with neem tree leaves to give musky fragrance and a few drops of cow's urine, which is considered pious for ritual purification as per Hindu philosophy, added to it. It was their first bath after the birth of the child. Both put new clothes brought by Tikamchand for the occasion. Balubai came out of the labour room for the first time holding her new born proudly and sat on the dais. *Panditji* put a *tilak,* the first worldly coronation, on the forehead of the child. Reciting the appropriate verses of the Vedas, he offered an oblation of *ghee* (clarified butter) in the fire prepared for this purpose.

Panditji consulted his almanac and suggested four names to the child, as per the date and time of birth, at the end of the ceremonial ritual. To choose a name was left to the discretion of Tolaram. Each of the women in the gathering turned to pray over the infant, entreating God to grant him long life, success in bringing credit and pride and many sons to the family, to village, and finally the strength and the spirit to deserve and to bring honour to the name he was about to receive. Jadaavbai thanked all with a packet of sweet and a handsome gift to *Panditji.*

The child thus basked every day in his mother's tenderness. Every morning Dhapa softened the baby's skin by greasing him from head to toe with mustard oil and butter repeatedly pressing his little head, nose, ears and lips, to shape them correctly. Mother and all callers started calling him by different names, "Bangu" "Haabu" etc.

The rest of summer weeks passed quickly and uneventfully. Toward the end of July one saw the gathering of the patches of clouds and the monsoon setting in. The trees became numb. No leaf stirred. There was intense drama in the way the suffocating stillness was broken by dark banks of clouds gathering as thunder rolled and lightning flashed across the sky. The fragrance of the earth and the excitement of soaking oneself in the rain enthralled the villagers, apart from healing the dryness and prickly heat of their body.

It was the month of September. Nights began to grow cold and the days were short. Rain had made every growing thing fresh and luxuriant. Balubai had recovered from childbirth and started doing her daily chore. Jadaavbai had long returned to her house in Calcutta, where her family carried their business activities. Soon the harvest season would start and Tolaram would join the family on Diwali, festival of lamps, for a long vacation. He would see his son soon.

Suddenly, events took a turn and hope turned into despair. A horrid telegram was received. (Telegrams were always considered horrid, because they brought bad news.) It was from Phoolwari announcing the death of Tolaram – a harsh blow of destiny.

The whole village stilled as the telegram reached there and for Balubai the day darkened outside and the whole world seemed to change as if all the happiness and support of life was about to be taken from her. The little paper had sent a bullet to the heart of Balubai. Gloom and agony fell all around and Balubai went in complete daze on receiving the news and sank into a state of despair and mental agony. Her husband was her life. Life became harsh to Balubai. She became a widow at a pretty young age. She was in her early thirties and Bangu only two and half months old.

It was a great shock to both the families. As per the customs, a widow should lead a life of solitude and need restrictions on her movement and clothing. Mala, who was only eight years old and Tolaram's pet—as she was his firstborn—could sense the seriousness of the time. She took Bangu in her arms and started caressing him. Bangu remained with his sister most of the time and he always fell asleep either Mala rocking him on her lap or bending on his bed singing softly.

The death of her son-in-law gave Dhapubai another shock. She could hardly overcome the shock of the untimely death of her elder son-in-law, Chhogmal, the husband of her elder daughter, Bhatubai. He died in Arakan, west Burma, some 3000 miles away from his native village, Malsisar. Her elder son Ranglal was in his early teens and was employed by the merchant, with whom Chhogmal was working so that Bhatubai could carry on his household of four sons, two daughters and a widowed mother left behind by her husband.

Family traditions and self-images, too, had their roles in shaping and forming values. A sense of self-respect prevented Balubai from bending and bowing. Balubai cherished deeply but quietly a sense of self-respect within her and someone has said that self-respect is the best quality human beings could have to fight the beast in themselves.

Balubai was aware of her responsibility towards her children. She wanted to bear the burnt on her own and assumed the difficult role of father-mother to her little flock. She grew tenderer and more approachable. The children loved Balubai as their dearest friend on earth. Her solacing black eyes had been their surest refuge in the trifling tragedies of childhood. She did not return to Tamkor after her brother Tikamchand, fetched her to Khinwasar, her parental home, subsequent to death of her husband.

At times it seemed to Balubai as if her son were trying to fill in for a man whom, she felt, he sensed was missing in her life. For a small boy, Bangu was so independent and self-sufficient and now or then when he got a cold or some small injury, he would set his mother smiling to herself with fantasies he'd share with her. At one year, Bangu was walking without assistance. By fifteen months he was even romping about clearly reveling in the sheer joy of being at last independent and on his own. She feasted her eyes on the boy waddling around, playing happily alone. Meanwhile, her two girls Mala and Para would go romping and skipping about, playing hide and seek and a few games they invented themselves.

Mala was now nine and Balubai became anxious about getting her married according to the tradition of the time. She started teaching her culinary affairs and other domestic skills so that she could adapt herself for a new life and in new home, where she would find new parents and a male companion, who would be strangers to her. Her marriage was fixed. Soon she would become a bride and would go away from her mother and brother. It was now Balubai's turn to assume the parental role and let her children not feel that their father was not in this world.

After a girl is grown up, her little brother now her

protector, seems like the big brother. Bangu was the man of the family now, which was a very important thing. Balubai got her son's nose and ears pierced so that he could put on gold rings, which her mother had gifted to the child on the day of his naming ceremony. *Nath*, rings, were put on his nose and ears. The boy, the cynosure of everyone's eyes, unknowingly got a name – Nathmal or *Nathu* – a catchy version of Nathmal in local dialect, so every near and dear started calling him "Nathu".

Women at that time could not have any property of their own except the jewellery given at their weddings. But Dhapubai bore her fate with great dignity and presented her children with an image of courage and a strong determination to ensure that they did not feel deprived of in any way.

Departing from one another is the way of the world, while meeting together is merely an ecstasy of the moment. Relatives of one's mother stand for indulgence and affection while those of one's father command respect and authority, convey a sense of authority and discipline.

Nathmal passed his first two and half years at Khinwasar with his mother and sisters. Both his sisters were blessed with saintly nature. Their mutual love, tranquillity and dignity, never expressed itself frivolously. A perfect parental harmony was the calm centre for the revolving tumult of four lives. Mala and Para had contrasting characters. Mala (Rosary) was calm, placid and self willed; while Para (Beloved), on the other hand, was effervescent, with a quality of impishness about her. His memories of these days had the quality of an evanescent dream.

Mala got married and was at her in-laws' house in

Kandua village near Rangoon, where they carried their family business. After Mala, their cousin Nanubai, the daughter of Pannalal, became a part of their establishment, making it again a unit of four.

Tolaram was very fair and tall. His sharp features accentuated his fairness and he looked strikingly handsome with broad chest and firm manly features. Nathmal remembered a picturesque description of his father dying although he was not an eye-witness at any stage of time or age, as he died when Nathmal was in infancy. This can be attributed to his virtue of the internal purity and had such transcendental experience that listening to him one felt a sense of magic and mystery.

Balubai looked frail, but she was always erect, active and had a great zest for life. She always awoke in the latter part of the night. Her day started observing *Samayika*, a temporary ascetic state of 48 minutes, to remain calm and undisturbed to discard all sinful activities and to engage in spiritual activities to be free of all passions, not to have feeling of liking or disliking, no attachment, no desire, no aversion.

During this period of sweet serenity, Nathmal would listen, half-asleep, to his mother reciting the *Chobisee*, the praise of 24 *tirthankars* and paying homage to their virtues and the *Bhikshu Chalisa*, hymn to Acharya Bhikshu, a profound Jain scholar of 18th century. This intensified in little Nathmal a love for Acharya Bhikshu.

After *samayika* Balubai busied herself with household chores while Nathmal slept some more. Ladies are considered fearful and weak. This impression is based on the basis of their physical structure. There are certain tasks which men do but the women can't, because their body composition being different, is not suitable for those exercises. It does not mean that they are inferior. They show courage where men develop cold feet. Balubai's piety, tolerance, patience and self-discipline were incredible. Self-discipline and tolerance makes one fearless.

Balubai was very possessive of her children. She would often call Nathmal and as he huddled close to her, eager and receptive, would sing sermons and tell stories, engrossing little Nathmal in tales of many Indian saints and the characters of the *Ramayana* and the *Mahabharata,* the great Indian epics.

Balubai devoted her spare time to sewing, singing Jain hymns and rested in the afternoon issuing stern commands to her children to remain inside the room during the afternoon and sleep. Nathmal conformed to this regimen but whenever he wanted to play he took his mother's permission. Afternoons were the time to play marbles with a group of boys he had befriended in the neighborhood. Those glass marbles in shades of red, yellow, blue and green were his most precious possessions.

In the evening the mother became the centre of their universe starting with the evening meals. The family had dinner usually before sunset. The children sat on mats, with their *thalis* placed on a wooden dais, in a row in the kitchen. Balubai served them from pots simmering on the *choolah,* a stove fired by wood and cow dungcakes. After dinner they sat around her and listened to her many stories, fables and family lore.

Nathmal saw his mother simply clad in *Ghaghra* and *Orhna,* a typical dress worn in Rajasthan and Gujarat, in colours prescribed for widows. Her dress made her a noble looking woman and the children thought the unfashionable clothing covered the most splendid mother in the world. While he would lie beside his mother Nathmal would ask her questions about religion and scriptures.

Nathmal asked his mother why, when other ladies perform many rituals and *tantras* for procuring divine favour by reciting charms and honorific titles of the deities, she always recited scriptures for *Arhats,* who are remote and unapproachable.

Balubai, stroking the hair off his forehead, would reply in a very lucid native dialect that the law of cause and effect *karma,* the sum total of human action without ethical connotation, applies to all lives. Even Gods are not exempt from law of retribution. One reaps what one sows. Each one has to attain freedom and perfection by one's own effort. No one, not even *Tirthankars,* supreme sanctified souls, can help him in attaining liberation.

Jainism is a religion of purely human origin and is preached and practiced by one who has attained perfect knowledge, omniscience and self-control by his own personal efforts and has been liberated from the bonds of worldly existence. Such human beings are considered Gods of Jainism.

The concept of God as a creator, protector, and destroyer of the universe does not exist in Jainism. Also the idea of God's reincarnation as a human being to destroy the demons is not accepted in Jainism. It is not an atheistic religion because it believes in many Gods who are self realized individuals and who have attained liberation. They question the attribution of qualities of omnipotence, omniscience, eternity and perfection to a God whose very existence is doubtful.

One argument says that the existence of God is based on inference, not perception, and knowledge derived from inference is doubtful. It needs to be confirmed by perception. The notion of God as Creator is rejected on the grounds that it presupposes that the universe is a product. But the universe according to Jains is eternal and so cannot be produced. God cannot be said to be omnipotent, for if it were so then he should be the cause of all things.

Jains also disagree on the unitary conception of God. The theists uphold the view that God is unique – that there is no one equal to, parallel to or like him. He has to be unitary for if it were otherwise and there were many gods, each one with his own plans, objectives and activities then the world would not be a harmonious world as in fact it is but would be one in which each of the gods may work at cross purposes.

Jains also reject the view that God is eternally perfect on the grounds that the term eternally perfect is an absurd locution. They argue that the quality of perfection is achieved by the removal of imperfections. So the attribution of this quality of perfection to a being, which was never imperfect, is a misuse of the term perfection.

However, the rejection of the belief that a God exists does not imply that Jains reject the existence of sublime spiritual and profound religious experience.

Jains do not lay emphasis on sacrifices, rituals, ceremonies but stress prayers and meditation on higher beings, liberated souls or *tirthankars,* considering them as highest spiritual ideals to which every soul can aspire. Jains neither seek mercy and forgiveness, nor indulge in self deprecation and confession of guilt. They seek guidance and inspiration from these liberated souls in their own quest for liberation. By meditating on the pure qualities of these great beings, each one can purify his own mind and heart, overcome the obstructing *karma,* work out his own salvation and therefore become a liberated soul.

The existence of *tirthankars* and meditating on them, like the aide memoir, just serves to remind one's potential for perfection. They serve as the source of inspiration and assurance of the efficacy of the method and practices, the rightness of the path and encourage treading the path to liberation. They serve as the paradigms, the role models.

Nathmal's home training had been so exacting. Nathmal could get his breakfast only after offering his salutation to the visiting Jain mystics in the village. It seemed to him, his every move drew Balubai's irritated finger snapping if, indeed, he would get a cuff on the head, if Balubai caught his eyes on anything except his own food. Unless he washed off every bit of dirt when he came into the home from a hard day's play, Balubai would snatch up her scratchy sponge and soap and make Nathmal think she was going to scrape off his very skin.

For him ever to stare at her or at any other adult, would earn him a slap as quickly as when he committed the equally serious offence of interrupting the conversation of any grown-up. And for him ever to speak anything but truth would have been unthinkable. Since there never seemed any reason for him to lie, he never did.

Though Balubai didn't seem to think so, Nathmal tried his best to be a good boy, and soon began to practice his home-training lessons with his sisters and other children. When disagreements occurred among them, as they often did – sometimes fanning into exchanges of harsh words and finger-snapping Nathmal would always turn and walk away, thus displaying the dignity and self-command that his mother had taught him were the proudest traits of the Acharya Bhikshu.

Nathmal was tremendously honest. His simplicity and silence became proverbial in the village. *Banias* are considered to be clever. Being simple and guileless had its price. He was taunted as *Buddhu* (village bumpkin). But he did not care for such remarks and did not think that he was really weird.

Balubai was very careful about his son's food. Nathmal had a sweet tooth. She prepared *pera,* a cookie prepared by condensing milk and mixing sugar with it, at home. She kept a cow to meet the milk requirement of the family. Balubai had her own underground reservoir of drinking water harvested during the rainy season. As per Jain practice, she made it *achit* (soft) by adding a small quantity of lime in the drinking water pot. This treatment causes clumping of bacteria and other foreign particles to settle out during several hours of sedimentation. The sludge is thrown away and fresh water is filled every morning. Jain monks are allowed to use only *achit* water.

Nathmal grew up strong and healthy, despite not playing any organized sports. Good air and water and regular meals were the secrets of his health.

Those were the days of rupee and anna. 16 annas made a rupee. It seems small by present standards, but it was a large sum for those days. One rupee could buy a family one month's grain and one anna the day's provisions. There were limited varieties of eatables and milk was the main dish.

Camel and camel carts were means of transportation in rural areas and only seasonal vegetables were available, which could be bartered for grains or old household articles. Everything was natural and vegetable ghee and inorganic fertilizers were yet to be invented. Ailments were cured by household remedies.

Means of living were simple and there were no electricity or water bills to upset the budget of a housewife. Balubai lived on with the income she received from the shop of her deceased husband, looked after by a *Munim* (caretaker) Surjoji Baman, and was very well satisfied with her lot. Somehow she did not let her children feel pinch of absence of their father. With a homemaker like Balubai even such a simple life was fulfilling, fulfilling the physical and spiritual needs

Nathmal had no formal education in a proper school. In those days teaching was a very low paid profession. Tamkor was devoid of any school. A wise man of late middle age and of limited means ran a school in his courtyard. He was known as Guruji. The school timings changed with the seasons and he usually took his classes on the ground, with children sitting on mats and the teacher on a stool.

Nathmal had his learning of the vernacular script and basic number skills, useful for the children of the community mainly engaged in commerce and finance, there. There were not many books and method of instruction was slate and chalk, which were the main educational implements. Writing on paper was done with grass quilt pens dipped in black ink made of bitter orange juice mixed with soot.

Guruji was in a habit of catching an occasional nap while

the children learnt by rote, reading aloud in a most terrific manner. If he found any child not learning his lesson he used to twist his ears, and dole out further punishment depending on the severity of the offence. There was neither examination nor progress report nor facility for games and sports.

Balubai occasionally visited her paternal home at Sardarshahar town, where Balubai's parents had migrated from Khinwasar in the course of time. She sent Nathmal to school whenever she was there and took him out of school when she returned to Tamkor. These scattered weeks of school attendance at Neminath Sidha, Sardarshahar, did not add to his learning.

Balubai was extremely fond of her son and could not bear even a day's separation from him. Nathmal was devotedly attached to her and admired her beyond measure. He felt secure in her company. It was his greatest happiness. He knew how much she was for him. He never thought of separation from her and could not endure it. Those were drawbacks, and kept him at home when he ought to have been at school.

Those days girls for the most part were unlettered and unschooled. People considered education as means of professions or service and girls were not educated, as a result women fell victim to illiteracy and consequent blind faiths. Girls would confine themselves to cooking, cleaning, knitting and pleasing the husband.

Balubai learned the alphabet at home but her conscientiousness and impeccable morals influenced her children. She considered that true education could be imparted only by the parents and gave the first place to the culture of the heart and of building character. Nathmal was a great model of obedience and Balubai complacently admired the success of her training that she hoped would stand her son in good stead when he took up the profession of his father. Yet so avid was he for learning that he taught himself to read by reading his mother's religious books. This gave him religious education that was refined by Jain sages and nuns visiting Tamkor from time to time.

To overcome her unhappiness and to cope with the loneliness within her and the wilderness outside she always kept Nathmal close by. Nathmal watched his mother performing her household chores—skimming curd or sewing and catering to the needs of the poor. But he remained troubled by unasked questions, the most obsessive being about his mother's tears and her loneliness.

Males stayed distant, but their presence gave him a feeling of security. Besides his mother he was looked after by his deceased father's brothers, who always remained a symbol of authority that he never dared question.

Nathmal was very close to his cousin, Mahalchand, the son of Gopichand. Mahalchand was married and his wife was equally good to him. Nathmal reposed complete confidence in no one but in the couple. He told everything to them. It came natural for him to do so and they had a deep concern in everything Nathmal told to them. He felt that he had all of their attention when he was with them. He esteemed and liked them.

One morning Nathmal suddenly heard the howling of a familiar voice from the direction of Gopichand's house. A chill shot through him, for it was the voice of his mother.

Nathmal was old enough to know that the howling meant a loved one had just died. Other women immediately joined in a piercing cry that soon spread all the way across the compound. Nathmal ran blindly toward Gopichand's house, from where the sorrowful cries were coming.

Amid the milling confusion, Nathmal saw an anguished Gopichand and his wife, Balubai, Mahalchand's wife and other ladies bitterly weeping. Numb with shock, Nathmal stood watching, as was the custom on the occasion of a death. No one seemed to notice Nathmal. Nathmal burst suddenly into tears, as much in fear as in grief. Soon men came with a large, bamboo logs and set it down in front of the house. Nathmal watched as the men brought out and laid on the bamboo's flat surface the body of Mahalchand, enclosed from neck to feet in a white cotton cloth.

Through his tears, Nathmal saw wife of Mahalchand taking seven rounds around dead body. After most of the mourners had dispersed away, Mahalchand's wife, his mother and other old women took up post nearby, huddling and weeping and squeezing their heads with their hands.

According to the custom of the forefathers, only the men of Tamkor, those who were able to walk, joined the procession to the crematorium, not far from the village, where otherwise none would go, out of the fearful respect for the spirits of their ancestors. The funeral pyre was built and the stiff, white-wrapped body was consigned to the flames and funeral rites were performed.

Afterward, for many days, Nathmal lost all joy, all hopes, all pleasure and hardly ate or slept, and he did not go anywhere with his mates. So grieved was he that Balubai, one evening, took him to his fold, speaking to his son more softly and gently than she ever had before, told him that none can share another person's sorrows. Death is surely going to overtake us. Just as hawk pounces upon the partridge and makes it bereft of life, so also when the lifespan of a person comes to an end, death snatches him from life. Young and old, even the child in the womb, are not spared by death.

The living body is born and will die but the soul in the contact of the living body is not born and will not die. Only souls who have attained *Nirvana,* and hence salvation can escape the illusory world of phenomena and cycle of rebirth or transmigration of soul, thus released from the rule of *Karma,* the sum total of past acts.

Nathmal listened to his mother entranced and asked who can attain *Nirvana,* Balubai clarified, "Origin of human sorrow, suffering and dissatisfaction is desire, which includes physical ambition, craving, longing and selfishness of all kinds. The means to its abandonment is detachment. *Nirvana* is a state of complete detachment which when attained permanently, brought cessation of rebirth. The spirituals adept who could achieve this goal are known as *Arahat* or *Arahant* (worthy)". A train of thoughts started on the nature of death and the seed of detachment constituted in the little mind.

Tamkor was not connected by a concrete road and the only means of transport were camel and camel carts, but along the network of walking paths between villages came enough visitors—passing by or stopping off in Tamkor. They included snake charmers, magicians, puppeteers, vagabonds, street singers, drama party, fakirs and all sorts of saints.

Nathmal was eight years old when one morning an old saint came to Balubai's door. He was barefooted and his soiled clothes and unshaven face gave him the appearance of a tramp. He was plump with dark skin and large gleaming eyes. His quick gaze rested on Nathmal.

Nathmal gave him water and a millet bread, the principal food of the region. Millet bread can be eaten without any supporting vegetable. Balubai always prepared extra pieces of bread for the poor coming to her door.

Balubai had been standing silent in the yard, within earshot. As the old saint left with a great smile on his face he told Balubai, "Mother! he has the sign on his brow, he has to become a great Yogi". It was in the same vein and style Nathmal heard him saying to his neighbour and boyhood friend that he would die after one week, but the face of the saint was devoid of any expression when he was saying so.

The news of the prediction spread in the village. No one took it seriously and nor did the death prediction have any sad affliction on the boy and his family. Rather the two boys became the laughing stock, though a few of villagers were looking at them strangely. The events of the subsequent week left the villagers stunned. The other child passed away.

The news of prediction and its part accomplishment spread like wild fire across surrounding villages. The affair was the talk of all and sundry. However, an earnest search did not help in tracing the saint out.

One's destiny is nature's secret. A *yogi*, an ascetic of high order, whose mind is calm, looks into the eyes of others and can read what is written on one's brow and can tell not only of the present but of the past and even the future easily. They need not study palms.

The word, *yogi* was new to Nathmal and he did not understand its meaning. It remained in his mind and acquired greater significance as he grew older.

Para was given in marriage at the age of 13 in the year 1928. In those days patriotism was the religion of every Indian and self-rule was the national objective. A movement was going on throughout the country to drive the British out of India. No individual or part of the country was aloof from the uprising.

A member or two of the Oswal clan went to England. The conservative Jains then protested their travel as sailing across the sea was meant as sin. In a tradition where one becomes untouchable simply by violating the rules about food, they were condemned as *Vilayati*, pro-British, and plagued by social ostracisms as it was the general impression that one could not live in Europe as a pure Jain ought to live, where vegetarians were dismissed as cranks. Englishmen were considered infidels.

The *vilayatis* countered that everything that happened in India—technology, science, education, colleges, universities, railway lines, telegraph, roads, cars, airplanes—happened because of the British rule. There was no way to be educated: the only educated people were the brahmins, because the father would teach the son. They kept everybody else uneducated because that was the best way to keep others enslaved.

Before the British rule, women were brunt alive with their husbands dead body. And this was all religious ritual for thousands of years. The credit goes to the British empire, that they prevented it; they made it crime. Karl Marx was not wrong when he said that religions have functioned as the opium to the people. We should take it in full spirit and accept what is good for us.

There were allegations and counter allegations. The war of words took a furious turn. The community got divided into two rival factions. The quarrel had grown to such an extent, and so deadly was the enmity between them, that it extended to the remotest kindred, to the followers and retainers of both sides, in so much that a married daughter could not go to her parents' house and if she were at her parents' house, she did not return to her husband.

Para's bridegroom's party became apprehensive that some member of bride's family had contacts with socially boycotted persons. Meals were ready to be served to them but they did not want to eat even a single morsel. They packed their bag and baggage and started getting their camel caravan ready to leave Tamkor. There was lot of running around to reconcile the situation. Balubai was playing a difficult role of mother-father. The mood of gaiety was turning otherwise.

Nathmal and others, being yet little children, paid no attention to what was going on among the adults. They were playing blindman's buff. Nathmal was blindfolded as his turn came. Suddenly, he struck something blunt and heavy on the forehead. He was bleeding from a gash between the two eyebrows over the body's master gland (pituitary gland).

There was bedlam. Adults were engrossed with the problem and each and every member of the marriage party was important to them and to attend to them was everyone's priority. They were doing their best and hardly having time to pay attention to Nathmal's weeping and crying with pain.

Balubai came to know of Nathmal's injury. To her, her son was her soul. She, leaving everything aside, rushed to the spot where he was crying. She calmed him down and applied turmeric powder in the cut in the middle of two eyebrows and bandaged an old cotton cloth around his head, while consoling saying, "His fortune has smiled on him. His *Divya Drishti*, a holy spot of man's consciousness, was operated upon by nature. His divine eye in the forehead opened up."

In the meantime the issue concerning the marriage party was resolved and they stayed back. Dinner was served to them. They became more cheerful and partook in the merrymaking. The remaining ceremonial ritual became more joyful. Nathmal became the centre of compassion for everyone. Their eyes feasted exultingly on him and said, "Fortune has smiled on you."

Nathmal's first glimpse of world came in his journey to Calcutta by rail. Nanubai's marriage was to be solemnized in Memonsingh, in Bangdesh (subsequently it was divided and this part is now known as Bangladesh) and enroute Balubai and Nathmal reached Calcutta.

It was a new world for Nathmal; no barking dogs; no howling donkeys; a lot of human beings. All sorts of automobiles were there on roads, in place of camels or camel carts. No Feuenhand or Dietz kerosene lanterns, no kerosene jewel lamps—Calcutta had piped water and electricity. Nathmal touched a switch on the wall and there was light. It was all quite miraculous. They stayed at the house of Jadaavbai. It was a multi-storied building, with lots of people lingering around the street.

Barabazar, was the largest merchandise centre in the

country. It had separate wholesale and retail markets for different items spread in large buildings, narrow lanes, streets and roads. Which lane, street or road leads to which place was mind boggling. There were plenty of people anywhere and no place was free from miscreants and cheaters. It was safer in the village than in Calcutta. One may get cheated, robbed and even murdered, if there was anything to be got by it.

Balubai, surprisingly, allowed her son to go to the market with his uncle Pannalal and Surjoji Baman with lots of admonition. They went from market to market making lots of purchases for the upcoming marriage.

Nathmal did as he was bidden. He followed them at exactly the same pace, did everything he was told, never complained and never spoke unless spoken to. They were leading when moving from shop to shop and Nathmal lagging behind as a shadow. Suddenly, they disappeared from his vision. He moved to and fro but did not see them. He found himself among the people unknown to him at an unknown place. He was lost. He did not know what to do, where to go?

Nathmal found himself helpless. He did not know the address of his aunt. All buildings were tall, looked huge fairy palaces of the capital city of British India (New Delhi was inaugurated in 1931 as the new capital of British India), a major industrial hub, chief port of eastern India, a great learning centre and a place of pride of many *yogis*.

Nathmal was wearing a gold chain and a watch, which were enough to attract miscreants towards him. He took them out and put them in his pocket, took a "U" turn and reached home. He passed the real test of his mettle. It sent a message to all and his villagers that he was not *buddhu* as he was called there. His uncle and party made an extensive search and finding him nowhere reported the matter to the police.

Balubai was wonder-struck seeing her son returning home alone. Nathmal narrated the incident to her mother. Her eyes remained wide opened. Exhilarated and astonished she was filled with pride for her son. She could say that with the grace of Acharya Bhikshu, a great tragedy was averted, and gave her son a big hug. He could feel her body trembling and knew, more than ever before in his life, how much his mother really loved him. His recollection was faultless and memory sinless.

After Nanubai's marriage, Balubai and her son returned to Tamkor. They were now only two persons in the house. It seemed a lonely, lifeless sort of house. No children frolicked in the courtyard. She realized now how helpful her daughters were in her daily chores. Now she had only to look after her son. She became more concerned about him.

To Nathmal home did not remain a very pleasant place because of his loneliness, except that his mother sanctified it. The long journey to the East brought many experiences and dreams to Nathmal. His opinion of himself was not favourable. He longed to read and write and better himself in every way. His stay in village did not trouble him before but it did trouble him now. It would not get him anywhere. Most of the children of his community had their plans for study or learning trading skills. Some of them had deserted the village and others would follow soon.

Then, before the rains of 1930, Muni Chhabilchand with his disciple Muni Moolchand came to Tamkor to stay there for the duration of the rains. Jain monastic code does not permit the monks and nuns to move from one place to another during the monsoon.

Balubai attended daily sermons and asked Nathmal to attend as well. Both Munis were wonderful teachers in every sense of the word. Their tone was so sweet that one would love to hear them immensely. Their teaching whetted Nathmal's appetite to learning and he heard sermons very attentively.

The Munis started taking classes for the children. They preached that physical existence is not everything. Sensuous enjoyments yield momentary pleasure but in return cause prolonged misery. By their very nature, they give maximum sorrow and minimum happiness. They are an obstacle to emancipation and a veritable mine of misfortune.

For living beings, four combinations are rare to obtain: human-birth, listening to scriptures, faith in *Dharma* and energy to practice self-control. Soul is our inner self, the part of us that never dies. The soul is the architect of one's happiness and sorrow. The soul on the right path is one's own friend and a soul on the wrong path is one's enemy.

The human incarnation of the soul is a rare privilege and should not be frittered away in the pursuit of physical pleasure and material gains. Human beings are seen as the best and the most perfect creations and this incarnation must be utilized by the soul to rid itself of worldly bondage.

Spiritual existence is more necessary. Our endeavour must be to not only to meet bodily requirements and good health but to seek out the meaning of life. Human birth is quite rare and invaluable and hence a man should make his choices wisely. *Moksha* or liberation can be attained only in the human birth. Even the demi-gods and heavenly beings have to re-incarnate as humans to practice right faith, right knowledge and right conduct to achieve liberation.

Moksha, liberation, salvation or emancipation of soul, is a blissful state of existence of the soul, completely free from *karmic* bondage, free from the cycle of birth and death. A liberated soul is said to have attained its true and pristine nature of infinite bliss, infinite knowledge and infinite perception. Such a soul is called *paramatman,* supreme soul or God. It is the highest and the noblest objective that a soul should strive to achieve. In fact, it is the only objective that a person should have; other objectives are contrary to the true nature of soul.

With right faith, knowledge and right conduct all souls can attain this state. *Sama Sutta,* canonical tenets, state that *Nirvana* or *moksha* is neither pain nor pleasure, neither suffering nor obstacle, neither birth nor death; neither sense organs, nor surprise, nor sleep, nor thirst, nor hunger; neither *karma,* nor quasi-*karma* nor the worry, nor any type of thinking which is technically called *Artta*—sorrowful, *Raudra*—cruel, *Dharma*—virtuous, and *Sukla*—prime.

Dharma and *viveka* or discernment differentiates human beings from other life forms. *Viveka* helps us to realize the true self or the nature of the soul. The soul assimilates *karmas* due to passions like anger, pride, deception and greed, which must be counteracted by cultivating *dharma. Dharma* consists of 10 traits, which have been equated with 10 stepping stones leading towards relishing this goal.

The *dharma* of the soul is: *Mardawa,* humility, which means gentleness of nature or the feeling of pride. Pride leads to immodesty and impropriety of conduct and so it should be shunned.

Arjava, purity, honesty and righteousness implies leading a life free of deceit and craftiness.

Satya, truthfulness is understanding and believing in the true nature and form of things. Being truthful and behaving ethically with fellow beings is what *satya* is all about.

Shauch, detachment, cleanliness or freedom from defilement involves keeping the soul free from the *kasayas* (passion) and other vices of the world. *Sanyama,* self-control, is practising moderation and abstinence in everyday life.

Tapa, devotional penance is leading the life of a recluse or hermit while keeping oneself engaged in meditation and study of religion.

Tyaga, renunciation, is to relinquish or to give away in charity; to donate one's material possessions and wealth willingly for the welfare of the needy.

Aparigraha, austerity, is applying self imposed limit for worldly possessions. Even the desire to have more material gains is kept in check through constant practice of *Aparigraha.*

Brahmacharya, continence, or celibacy means maintaining chaste, moral behavior under all circumstances.

One who swims along with the current of the worldly life is entangled in the cycle of birth and death. One, who swims against it, gets liberated. That which is the most difficult to acquire and which is transient like the flash of lightning, if such human birth is wasted carelessly by a man, he is an unworthy person and not a noble man. One, who does not endeavour to tread the path of righteousness in this birth, repents at the time of death.

Both the Munis found Nathmal quite receptive and as a

further step started teaching him about nature and its relation to human life, which is the basis of Jainism, known as *Nine Tattvavas*. Jain metaphysic is based on nine truths or fundamental principles.

Two types of substances known as *Jiva,* living and *Ajiva,* non-living i.e. soul and *pudgal,* everlasting, uncreated, independent and co-existing categories pervade the entire universe. This can roughly be compared with the modern division of nature into organic and inorganic. All souls are equal and alike in their inherent nature, essential qualities, intrinsic characteristics and potentialities; they are capable of attaining liberation. The soul of ant and of an elephant is equal.

There are countless *jiva,* organisms, at different stages of personal evolution. They are of two types. They are mobile bodies ranging from bacteria to human, from infernal to celestial beings. They can walk of their own. They can resist and have two to five senses. The immobile *jivas* are single sensed and in the form of earth, fire, water, air and vegetable bodies. They can neither resist nor walk.

The soul is differentiated from non-soul or non-living reality that consists of: matter, time, space, medium of motion and medium of rest. The unity of soul with body is life. All living beings are made of above-mentioned two substances, *jiva* and *ajiva.* But this unity is a mark of continuity of *karma* body with soul.

Any act done with an ego, attachment or aversion, puts us under the influence of passion or intense emotion — anger, attachment, jealousy, pride and so on, termed as *Kasayas,* sticky substances — different accessories of *pudgal* are drawn towards our soul and transform into *karma. Karma* is also termed as *pudgal*. It is very fine and subtle matter and cannot be preceived or discerned by senses. *Karma* may be meritorious and demeritorious and called *Punya* and *Pap*.

Karma covers the soul just as a layer of dust quickly settles on a sticky surface. The influx of *karma* is called *asrava* and the resultant bondage is called *bandh*. It is possible to stop the influx of *karmas, sanwar* by maintaining equanimity and detachment as well as modify or shed the *karmas, nirjara,* through austerities and purity of conduct and intentions and negation of desires.

When the soul gets purified, or all the *karmas* get detached from the soul, this is known as *moksha,* complete deliverance almost liberation or state of salvation in Christianity. When the *karmas* are fully destroyed, the soul has its true nature, which includes infinite knowledge, infinite vision, infinite power and infinite excellence.

The soul liberated from the bondage of *karma* also gets liberated from transmigration. Each soul is one complete whole in itself, is eternal, immortal and retains its individuality even in liberation.

Lesson on the nine categories of cardinal truth gave Nathmal an understanding of: What is the universe like? Who am I and from where have I come and where I have to go? What is his true nature? What is non-living? What is the relationship between living and non-living? How can I remove impurities from myself?

It was clear to him that his real identity is soul and the soul is the slave of the body. He was made to understand that consciousness characterized by vision, knowledge and bliss is the intrinsic qualities of the soul. Form, sound, darkness, lustre, reflection, hot effulgence, colour, taste, smell and touch are the characteristics of non-living beings.

Soul is its own regulator – other than it or outside it, no body is its controller. The elements of bondage and salvation are inherent in it. It can choose anyone. *Karmas* are fruit bearing but if the soul is awakened, they will be dissipated without bearing fruits. Soul must decide that its true nature is quite different from that of the body and the worldly objects, which ultimately it has to settle in its true nature finally renouncing all wanderings in the not-self.

The fundamental knots of bondage and action are three – attachment, hatred and ignorance. Ignorance associates the soul with actions. Therefore ignorance is compared with darkness. Attachment and hatred are raised by ignorance and they enshackle the soul in the worldly cycle of birth and death.

Ignorance is destroyed by knowledge as darkness is dispelled by light. The light of the real nature of the soul will destroy the darkness of soul's ignorance. At the dawn of knowledge the soul and the *pudgal* appear in their true colours and a realization of the soul, as quite distinct from and unrelated to the body, results. That by which these three knots can be loosened and destroyed is the path to liberation.

One should devote one's time to acquiring knowledge and meditation and thereby save oneself from the bondage of fresh actions.

The path of liberation of the soul from sufferings and realization of its full powers followed by the pure and holy Muni Moolchand and Muni Chhabilchand and preached to Nathmal started shaping the mindset of Nathmal. His inner personality opened up and his life was not lacking a direction.

Heredity alone does not shape one's consciousness in a deterministic way. Reflecting on the teachings of Munis, a stream of amazing detachment arose in him. "I am much more ignorant than I considered myself. I need to find my own worth and the way to myself."

Every individual who wishes to rise above his existing level needs a lighthouse, a guiding star to guide him on the journey of life which can help by dispelling darkness at every step.

Once the right path is decided, one should start acting up to it, and not remain in an unhappy state of doubt and indecision. Nathmal had been betraying signs of disenchantment from the material world and rise of spiritual feelings. He made up his mind to take up the path of spiritual discipline.

Balubai was grieved as he softly revealed his resolve to remain celibate all his life and go out to seek the true peace for spiritual pursuit to his mother.

Mother's eyes were quick to see any change in the mind of her child and holding his hand and watching his face wistfully she staged a mock rebuke and admonished that it was hard to observe the renounced life. A monk has to hold forgiving and other attributes; he has to protect them vigilantly. He has to maintain equanimity towards friends and foes, has to maintain identical attitude towards himself and others and thus for the entire universe.

It is too hard to observe five major restraints together with the restraints of not taking food at night and also to bear 22 afflictions, like hunger, thirst etc. He is of very tender age. As such she advised him to resort to religious life in old age.

Balubai knew her son's mind well and thought that any persuasion would be of no avail. She could never make him do what he did not want to do. He was so stubborn. And he could not be talked out of what he wanted to do. He was so determined. Sometimes it drove her mad.

The mother sensed change in her son's attitude. There was no use to try to be hard with him. She did not try to be hard to him. She seemed to have lost all the will to fight. The thought of separation from her son started paining her. His decision created a lot of excitement and she needed a counsel for herself and his son to get out of this predicament. She could not sleep well in the nights.

Nathmal was blithely unaware of the trouble he had caused to his mother. He saw the helplessness in his mother's eyes, and also the love. He saw how torn she was and he felt awful for tearing her. But he did not lose his calm and looked on with approved favour.

Following the patriarchal Indian custom, Tolaram's brothers were the natural guardians of Nathmal. His grand parents had also died. He approached Balchand to allow him to initiate on spiritual path. Balchand ridiculed his plan as religious fanatic and engaged Nathmal in a lengthy philosophical discourse. He discountenanced his idea of being a monk and tried to dissuade him from assuming path of spiritual discipline, saying, "If you desert your ordinary responsibilities, you would meet continual misfortune. One cannot work out his past *karma* without worldly experience. You are protected from pain, grief and despair by your mother. On the way pebbles and thorns would hurt your feet and that could result in bleeding. You had solely indulged in playful games. One can become a Muni by tonsuring but you are always busy with a mirror and comb".

Nathmal, who was shy and reticent but enlightened replied, "The soul is independent and generally none is really related to the other. The soul itself is the author as well as destroyer of joy and sorrow. The soul pursuing the right path is a friend, while that going astray is an enemy. It is not hard to observe monastic code for those, who have no inclination for objects of sense. Pain is to body and not to soul. He could show him he is able to bear the pain of uprooting his hairs." (A Jain monk is not allowed to use any tool to shave off hairs.)

He quoted that he goes on foot 10 miles to his *massi,* (mother's sister), house in Malsisar. When in distress, a person has to experience his miseries all alone. After death he goes to the next life all alone. Hence it is not wise to consider anyone worth taking shelter under.

Mere birth in Jain family does not mean that one will obtain liberation. One has to work for what one believes. One whose soul practices religion will gain by it. But the forceful prognostications of Balchand had slightly shaken Nathmal's confidence. Balchand did not give him permission perhaps in order to time test depth of his determination and went away to his place of business in Bangdesh, urging him to put his brain in trading skill.

Such a situation would have provoked Nathmal and he would have lost his control over his anger and his way of passive resistance was giving up food. When he could not bear hunger and found his mother ignoring him, he stood up holding a pillar or a door as was his habit.

His process of self realization got a momentum and Nathmal became closer to enlightenment. He withdrew completely within himself and immersed in deep austerity. He became oblivious of all worldly affairs. He turned his back to all worldly pleasure and dear objects easily available to him, such as good food, good bed etc. Balubai used to remain charmed by observing his calm, quiet, ascetic and brilliant appearance.

It was early morning and Balubai woke her son and told him that they would be going to Malsisar. Her elder sister Batubai was her great mentor. To her she was her mother in distress. Her elder son, Ranglal, was of discernible wisdom beyond his age. He was earning a livelihood for the family in Calcutta, but at that time he was available in Malsisar.

Nathmal knew his *massi's* home from Tamkor so well that he could walk it with his eyes closed. He had a great regard for Ranglal and became anxious to see his cousin. Batubai was very happy to see her sister and nephew. It was a great union of two sisters. They discussed everything in detail.

Balubai returned from Malsisar with a consolation that if Nathu has decided to renounce all worldly hopes, she should also take a road away from worldly ambitions. She realized that her affection and attachment were based on ignorance. Where there is no attachment, there is no resentment. Attachment is the cause of acute bondage of *karma*. Husband and son, friends and relatives live with a person as long as she/he is alive. None accompanies after death. The pain of life can be shared neither by fellow members of the sect/caste, nor by friends and kith and kin.

One has to suffer pain alone when it stares him in the face. *Karmas,* actions, chase the agent only and none else and that life is ephemeral. One should reflect thus : "One day I have to abandon all the wealth and property, land and estates, gold and ornaments, children, relatives and friends and even my own body." To fulfil one's earthly responsibilities is indeed the higher path, provided the *yogi,* maintaining a mental involvement with egotistical desires.

Balubai was born and bred up in the Jaina religious tradition and remained involved in *dharamdhyan,* religiously oriented meditation, and did not see any hurdle in her way, the destination of *karma,* a path of liberation.

It was a total disintegration of the family, started in September 1920 after the death of her husband. Mala had gone, Para gone, Nanu gone and now it was the turn of her son. Balubai did not think that it would come so soon but she would not stop him.

Balubai sounded out Balchand and Pannalal. She informed her daughters Mala, Pyari and Nanu of their decision, a decision taken by the mother and her son jointly. She asked them to take charge of everything, the house she got as her share, business of her husband and every material thing and let them free from worldly bondage.

With the blessing of Muni Chhabilchand both mother and son set out for Gangashahar, where Acharya Kalugani, eighth religious head of Terapanth sect, tall and thin was staying. He was a combination of perfect purity and perfect learning.

Acharya Kalugani received them cordially. They told him the purpose of their visit. Acharya Kalugani found in Nathmal a true seeker, who did not swerve from truth. He was authentic so he did have courage to face any difficulty of monkhood way of life. The Acharya gave his permission. Nathmal's heart overflowed with gratitude. For his mother (Balubai) Acharya kept his decision in abeyance. This made little Nathmal very puzzled. He was unwilling to accept monkhood leaving his mother in the lurch.

Nathmal requested the revered Acharya again and again. Acharya was impressed by Nathmal's tenacity and acceded to initiate Balubai into his congregation. Process of total detachment accelerated. Mother was overwhelmed by feeling that her son's worldly duties were diluting and was filled with a presentiment that foretold that one day he would be a glorious Acharya.

Balubai and Nathmal returned to Tamkor after the announcement of date of their *Diksha,* swearing ceremony. Both were asked to learn *Pratikarman,* atonement and an exercise of introspection, mindfully examining one's faults, repenting for that and turning back from the same.

Pratikarman is a form of meditation where one reflects on his spiritual journey and renews his faith. It takes the form of periodic meditation. It is undertaken in *Kayosagga,* detachment from the body by controlling it, patiently, vigilantly and with mental concentration in a language that one can understand. It humbly lays friendship for the entire universe. *Pratikarman* includes, stay in equanimity by withdrawing to the self, prayers to superiors and Acharya, reflections on vows and past transgressions and making resolutions for the next period.

It can be summed that *Pratikarman* is the critical and analytical process of auditing of all the transactions conducted by the soul. It is an internal process of refining the character and behaviour to make it simple and good.

The 12th February, 1931 was the most memorable day in the life of Nathmal and so also for Balubai. Winter was at its fag end. It was a day of gaiety and Tikamchand prepared a festival for the occasion. The house at Sardarshahar was decorated abundantly and a feast was organized.

Numerous relatives from distant places came to Sardarshahar. Malu, and Para came from their in-laws house. There were also a large number of members of the Choraria clan from Tamkor and Batubai with her sons and grandsons from Malsisar. Nanubai, Balubai's sister, who was married at Sardarshahar, was very happy to have all them in Sardarshahar. All were in a festive mood and the mother and the son were filled with steady determination to undertake great renunciation.

As per tradition, Nathmal was dressed like a bridegroom in Sherwani and Jodhpuri turban with a feather plume, a dagger with red silver sheath and belt hanging from his shoulder. His Jaipuri walking boots made a very romantic cracking sound. This made him looked like a prince of fairy tales. The childhood slipped to boyhood.

Balubai's greatest desire was the marriage of her son. "Ah when I would behold the face of Nathu's wife, I shall find heaven on this earth", she expressed these words in her strong sentiment of family continuity.

Nathmal came to her mother for the final salutation. She could not believe her eyes. How fast his son had grown up. He looked like his father when he came to marry her.

She could not restrain her emotions. Her heart did overflow with motherly love. They looked into each other's eyes, where tears were shining. She pressed Nathmal to her bosom.

Balubai got separation from him with her last minute advice that now Acharya was your guardian and you firmly resolve to behave as advised by him and follow that resolve. She was extremely fond of him and could not bear even a day's separation from him. It was a great sacrifice of love of a mother, who nurtured her son with great affection and pinned all her hopes in him. It was incredible spirit of sacrifice. Her sacrifice made her the leader of non-violence.

The procession for oath taking ceremony of monkhood started following a band party and an Indian orchestra. Nathmal was on horseback behind the band, children, gents and ladies in their fineries and ornaments displaying their best, chanting hymns in the last making it pageantry of rare occasions in Sardarshahar, a remote town in Rajasthan known for its wealthy merchants and their *havelis*. Nathmal enjoyed himself riding through the streets full of onlookers on its both sides and ladies watching standing at the top of the roof of their *havelis*.

Revered Acharya Kalugani initiated the mother and the son to monkhood and admitted them in his congregation. A new relationship of guru-disciple was established by *diksha*. He, who looks at both straw and gold alike, is said to be truly initiated.

The Acharya bestowed on them the formal vows of the monkhood and they accepted the five major restraints of practice and unfailing observance of moral values (including of non-violence, honesty or truth, chastity or non-greed, non-possession and abstention from theft of both tangible and intangible) as a code of conduct to purify their souls from *karma*.

Mahavira put a very high value on silence. A Jain monk is called *muni,* which means 'the silent one'. He should withdraw his thoughts from sensations and be silent within. Nathmal became Muni Nathmal and his mother Sadhvi Baluji of the Terapanth order.

Terapanth is non-idolatrous and very finely organized under the complete direction of one Acharya, who is religious supreme. It is characterized as a highly disciplined order.

Monks revise the vows of obedience every evening facing the direction in which Acharya is moving along with his entourage spreading the religion. Muni discipline requires its members to obey their superior even when this entails grievous sin.

Monks should also observe three *Guptis,* controlling the physical, vocal and mental faculties. Three *guptis* help a sage to stay aloof from immorality just like a boundary debar wild animals away from a farm house. The flow of *karmas* into the soul is caused by the activities of body, speech and mind: so it is quite necessary for the ascetics to keep these channels of influx under strict control.

The three *guptis* are regulation of mind in such a way as to give room only to pure thoughts, of speech in observing silence for a particular period or in speaking only as much as is absolutely necessary and of speech; and of bodily activity, with reference to controlling inner nature, that is, they are dictated by the principles of self-control.

Monks should also observe five *Samities,* meticulous

care while undertaking any activity i.e. eating, speech, wish, exchange and discharge. It is just possible that even in performing the duties of an ascetic; the vows might be transgressed out of inadvertence. Hence as a precautionary measure the acts of carefulness are prescribed to cultivate the habit of carefulness in accordance with the principles of non-violence.

The *samities* are prescriptions for the regulation of walking, so as not to injure any living being, mode of speech with a view to avoid the hurting of other's feelings by the use of offensive words; eating food in a prescribed manner and especially with a view to avoid faults, actions of taking or using, and of putting away, of his accessories of scriptures, etc; of the movements connected with the answering of call of nature, i.e. he should be careful while handling their flywhisks, water gourds and disposing of bodily waste matter.

A Muni should be true to his oath throughout his lifespan and preserve his "equanimity", devoid of attachment and aversion and to be indifferent to life and death, gain and loss, fortune and misfortune, friend and foe, joy and sorrow. To develop the capacity to face both favourable and unfavourable circumstances with equanimity in religion.

A sage should keep himself busy in study of scriptures. The scriptures serve as a very useful means for getting rid of the defiling instincts and for becoming worthy. Incourteous language is against religion. Muni should never utter anything which lacks probity, which is categorical and capable of hurting others.

Munis do not take anything not properly given to them.

They observe celibacy and do not enjoy material happiness. They do not keep any possessions, which are not useful in their religious activity. They have also given up relationships and attachment to their families and friends. They would perform meditation, and live a pious life. They would voluntarily suffer many hardships to get rid of their *karma.* The sages do not touch or sit close to nuns, ladies, or girls and nuns do not touch or sit close to sages, men or boys. Both saints and nuns stay in separate places.

Munis would wear white clothes. They keep a few clothes, a few bowls to collect food and a *Mukhapatti,* a small piece of white cloth folded in a particular way, used in front of the mouth. Because of *mukhapatti* one becomes careful about what he/she speaks. It stops him/her from lying, and making provocative and non-beneficiary speech to others. One controls his/her speech, and speaks only when necessary. Uncontrollable spits are stopped by *mukhapatti* from falling on instruments of knowledge such as books. Insentient and warm air that is coming out of mouth is also stopped from mixing with sentient and cold air of the outside. By use of *mukhapatti,* one becomes humble and courteous.

A muni carries a *Rajoharan,* (soft broom) to be used to gently clean the floor to make the space free of subtle living beings. Its spiritual meaning is to remind us that we need to clean our soul of all *karma* particles. Bathing is forbidden as a part of nine-fold fence of celibacy. Muni should sleep on hard floor. They do not use padded and comfortable seats, such use being indicative of lack of self-control and desire for enjoyment. Muni is refrained from cleansing the teeth and taking food standing. He should avoid treading on growing plants, should never leave a vessel filled with a liquid substance uncovered.

Muni, who constantly moves on, remains pure like water that flows and never remains in one place longer than a month in order to avoid any growth of attachment. They walk barefoot so that they do not hurt bugs or insects. They should not eat and drink from sunset to sunrise. They do not cook for themselves and do not eat any food that is cooked especially for them. They eat only vegetarian food and refrain from all types of addictive substances such as alcohol and drugs.

They should not eat, drink, or wear any product made by hurting, torturing or killing animals, such as leather, silk. They should revise *Pratikarman,* every evening. They do not keep money, jewellery, or own anything, such as a house or a vehicle.

The following day Muni Nathmal visited the house of Tikamchand with his alms' pots. Tikamchand offered obeisance and touched the feet of Muni Nathmal in great reverence and proferred the first alms. Muni Nathmal did not take full offering and obliged Tikamchand with a very little of it after checking whether it was prepared for them. No Jain monk is permitted by his scriptures to take food especially prepared for him; he is only a recipient of what is superfluous and can easily be spared by the householder for the other's use.

All who were present there greeted Muni Nathmal with folded hands and in an entreaty mode while every male kneeling touched his feet in reverence and all completed salutation by saying, *Mathen Vandami,* I solemnly bow my head down.

□

II

JAINISM, traditionally known as Jain Dharma/Shraman Dharma, is simple and natural, yet its contribution in the philosophical field has been profound. Jain thinkers did not limit their world by preconceptions and kept on knowing the way things really are and saw the universe to be eternal working by its inherent laws and continues. There is nothing paranormal in the universe, except our limited understanding of nature and miracles and divinity are the fitments of human mind. It is the correct appreciation of nature, man and God. God is just a natural part of universe.

Jains follow the teachings of twenty four *Tirthankaras,* conquerors of their own selves, and victors over their senses, passions and desires, who reinstated the religious order at various times. They prescribed the same way of life as they had practiced – an unqualified path of personal purification and realization of the soul's true nature by self-improvement – and thereby reached perfection.

The philosophy given by Mahavira and by the earlier *Tirthankaras* is called Jainism. Jaina means a follower of "Jina".

Jainism contains the traces of the earliest developments of philosophical thinking in the history of mankind. The finds of figures of Jaina seers in the *kayosagga* postures in the excavations of Harappa and Mohanjodaro offer convincing support that Jainism is a pre-vedic religion which flourished in India even before the advent of the Aryans to India. These excavations are said to be more than 4000 years old.

The historical details of the first twenty-two *Tirthankaras* have been lost in the antiquity, and the available sources of information do not provide hope of recovering them. The lives and teachings of the last two *Tirthankaras*, Parshvanath (872 to 772 BC) and Mahavira (599 to 527 BC), are historical facts. From their times onwards, we get an accurate outline of the growth of Jain religion and philosophy.

Mahavira was a senior contemporary of Buddha. He was known by the name, "*Nigrantha* (without any ties – external or internal) *Natputra*" by the Buddhas.

Mahavira was more of a reformer and propagator of an existing religious order. However, Mahavira did reorganize the philosophical tenets of Jainism to correspond to his times. Mahavira was a philosopher as well as a *Tirthankara*. He made his enquiries in order to solve the problem of life and gave a new revelation to the religion preached by his predecessors.

Throughout its history, the Jain philosophy remained unified and single, although as a religion, Jainism could not keep it aloof from onslaught of division into various sects and traditions. Acharya Bhikshu was a great Jain scholar and interpreter of teachings of Mahavira. He made conventions so that these could be followed unerringly. Acharya Kalugani was the eighth religious head of venerable Terapanth order. Acharya Bhikshu was its first religious head and founder. Terapanth was founded in 1760.

Muni Nathmal's daily life in the congregation of Acharya

Kalugani flowed smoothly infrequently varied. Acharya Kalugani awoke before dawn and so his team. A man grows in the footstep of his father. There is a similarity in the life of Acharya Kalugani and Muni Nathmal. Both lost their fathers while they were in infancy. Acharya Kalugani lost his father when he was only three and half months old. Muni Nathmal continued to get love from the Revered Acharya and did not feel a vacuum created on separation from his mother. Acharya's wish was his law.

Sadhwis visited their Acharya on a turn basis or Acharya took their class from time to time. Whenever, *Sadhwi* Baluji came for *darshan,* the blessing which flows from mere sight of a saint, of Acharya Kalugani, Muni Nathmal put everything aside, gazed her ardently, vocal chord lost its all vibration and dropped it only on her turning towards him on ceremonial enquiry of his well-being. "Attachment to bodily residence, springing up of its own nature, i.e., arising from roots, or past experience of death," Patanjali wrote, "is present in slight degree even in great souls."

Acharya Kalugani commonly called him Nathu and out of affection also called him by his childhood pet names, Bangu and Habbu. A new name, 'Valkalchiri' was the epithet conferred on him for the innate purity, simplicity, sincerity, truth and morality of a simple rural folk, which was very pleasing to Acharya Kalugani.

Valkalchiri, a legendary character, was a jungle boy, who gained the final goal of *Kaivalya* (kewal Jnan), only knowledge. In this state, knowledge is not acquired through senses, i.e., acquiring knowledge is not a process. This state is like a mirror in which knowledge of all reality in space and time reflects and which thus ends all ignorance and curiosity that are prerequisites for acquiring knowledge.

Valkalchiri's father became a monk and abandoned his wife before Valkalchiri was born and never returned. Valkalchiri's mother died in childbirth and his upbringing was haphazard. The orphaned kid was found by sages clothed (*Chiri*) in *Valkal,* bark of a tree. Thus they started calling him Valkalchiri.

Once Valkalchiri lost his way in the jungle and was found by a merchant, travelling with his wife in a horse drawn chariot. Seeing horse, boy said deer was very large. Merchant's wife gave him some sweets to eat. The boy said to her, "Sir, the fruits are very tasteful." Finding his wife puzzled with his reply, the merchant clarified that this boy has been brought up in a remote hermitage, where he did not see any lady.

Balubai taught Nathmal to be truthful. Nathmal was an authentic seeker of truth and another Valkalchiri. Acharya Kalugani with his uncanny insight recognized these traits in him at a very early stage and groomed him for important roles for the service of humanity. He inculcated a new way of life and crafted his skill in such a way. Acharya Kalugani taught him that a spiritual practitioner should walk, stand, sit, sleep and speak with vigilance, circumspection, prudence and care all taken together so that he may not be bound by sinful actions.

Acharya Kalugani took extra care for his physical fitness and hygiene. There was change in meal order of Muni Nathmal. Revered Acharya looked whether famishment gleamed in his eyes. Whether he got his share of alms? Whether he had proper clothes, how he wears them. He himself demonstrated the way of wearing *pachhewadi,* a seamless cloth, put around the body by saints.

Acharya Kalugani watched his steps and taught him how to walk. When Acharya Kalugani passed his comments on his handwriting he reckoned his wish and improved it. He always remained on a look out as to what was wish of his Guru.

One cold winter morning in the rural desert town of Chhapar (Rajasthan), where winter is severe, Muni Nathmal went out to bring homeopathic medicine for one of his fellow Munis in the absence of Acharya Kalugani. When Acharya Kalugani returned he did not find Muni Nathmal and was very much puzzled when he came to know that he forgot to take his warm shawl with him. Acharya Kalugani asked two of his mates to take his warm shawl to him and make sure that he puts it.

Muni Nathmal was overwhelmed when he received the shawl on his way from his co-Munis. Both his co-Munis handed over the shawl to him with their mischievous twinkle in their eyes, but only praised magnanimous action of Acharya and for his affection for Muni Nathmal. Such heart warming acts of Acharya made a deep impression on Muni Nathmal and he admired him and his faith in him strengthened, which intensified his devotion and broadened his outlook.

Muni Nathmal was sent to Muni Tulsi to study Jain scriptures. It was his second meeting with Muni Tulsi. Their first meeting at Gangashahar, where he went along with his mother to seek permission of Acharya Kalugani for *Diksha* was momentous. It was a special instruction of Muni Moolchand to him to call on Muni Tulsi, who was in very good books of Acharya Kalugani.

At first glance, Nathmal found Muni Tulsi a charming youth with wide forehead and abstracted eyes of a dreamer. They were full of lustre and steadiness. They declared the single-mindedness of his purpose. His face was smiling and in full bloom. It clearly declared the internal joy and peace.

Muni Tulsi smiled at Muni Nathmal graciously. Nathmal was so young that he did not know how to give expression to his feelings, but in his heart he was hoping that he would offer to be his teacher. He read his thought. Conversation was just civility to his asking for his name, place from where he hailed and purpose of the visit. The meeting truly became dynamic—an intimate, loving exchange between the souls in the sanctuary of silence within. In Muni Tulsi he found a combination of perfect purity and perfect learning.

Now Acharya Kalugani was his spiritual master and Muni Tulsi was his teacher. In general the students have less love for the teacher; he is considered a source of fear, dislike and uneasiness. Under his noble command he could pursue his study. He had to obey his strict discipline. Acharya Kalugani was more approachable than Muni Tulsi.

The basic principles of Jainism are scientific and the truths presented in the scriptures are universal, however, their interpretations and applications have to be done in the context of time and space in which we find ourselves. The teachings of Mahavira are preserved in *Agama*. *Sidhanta* or *Agama* and *Sutras* are elder monuments of Jainism and have come down to us through a very rich tradition. The common people of India were speaking and writing languages that were simpler than classic Sanskrit. The oldest *Sutras* of the Jain are written in Awadh Magadhi, verses and prose. The sacred texts, *Sidhanta* or *Agama* employed Prakrit.

The first text book given to Muni Nathmal was *Dasavaikalika Sutra,* a manual of discipline for monks, which contains 210 detailed conventions of ritual purification. Its knowledge helps strengthen faith in the imperatives of the Jain monastic rules. Its language is Prakrit.

Acharya Kalugani asked Muni Tulsi to start teaching Sanskrit, the base academic language of ancient Indian moral discipline, to new monks side by side. There was emphasis on committing the text to memory than understanding and recite them to develop a good memory. It required a lot of disciplined practice.

Without developing memory one cannot become a well-educated person. By improving the quality of memory, we can make it powerful enough to remember all things. It has been proved that many mental deficiencies may be overcome by the practice of concentration exercises. Both the languages were totally new to the village folk, who spoke native dialect so far. He sought every opportunity to forsake prosaic grammar and indulged in talk with his colleagues in the absence of Muni Tulsi.

Muni Nathmal was in the threshold of childhood when he became a Muni. His new career demanded careful routine but his childish instincts were not developed and he enjoyed childish pranks and freaks. He gave full vent to his innate inclination in support of those of Muni Budhmal.

Muni Budhmal was his intimate companion for he was of his age and hailed from a rural town near his village.

Both accepted the monkhood in the same year. He was his true ally. The obedient disciple could comprehend fully the countenance of the Acharya when it was brought to his notice and before condemnation could get words, Acharya Kalugani could grasp the assurance that it would not be repeated. Nathmal's expression gave Acharya Kalugani all the answers he needed.

Once Acharya Kalugani received two identical woollen blankets as alms in the presence of Muni Nathmal. One of them was having a black spot. He wanted to give one blanket to Muni Nathmal and the other to his co-Muni, Muni Budhmal. Muni Nathmal insisted that he be given the one which did not have the spot. Before the insistence turned into obstinacy, Acharya Kalugani gave it to Muni Budhmal

Acharya Kalugani conveyed him a lesson – not through words, shrugging of shoulders or a look of eyes, but in his absolutely neutral countenance. Message was well received by Muni Nathmal. Nothing is worse than a go with gravitation. Pleasure is nothing better than renunciation of the same. To sacrifice everything for others is real monasticism. Non-violence and insistence are non co-existent. If you give up your small self for the sake of others you will not only find your real self, but will also make others your own. The more you seek to save your little self, the more you lose your true self and estrange others.

Muni Tulsi wrote a poem for Muni Nathmal and others, to be sung on the occasion of "Maryada Mahotasva", an annual assembly. He did not like it and told Muni Tulsi that it was not good. In spite of repeatedly told to him by Muni Tulsi that it was equally good to one he had written for the other monks. Muni Nathmal did not agree to it and Muni Tulsi told him that in future he would not write any poetry for him. It gave Muni Nathmal a chance to try his hands at poetry and he wrote good poetry. He received lot of praises for his poetry and Acharya Kalugani awarded him the first prize.

There were five-six students to whom Muni Tulsi was teaching. Whenever, Muni Tulsi was away for some work, they indulged in the usual pranks, guffaw or gossip and incurred severe reprimand of Muni Tulsi for their unprofessional behaviour. It did not have any effect on them. One of them would sit at the gate as guard to alert others on Muni Tulsi's arrival. This did not help them learn the lesson and Muni Tulsi reached at the end of his patience. He meted punishment to them, which included standing for a period of time, foregoing breakfast, to stop giving them further lesson and made them devoid of all freedom.

Munis felt suffocated by excessive discipline. This made them very uneasy. Muni Budhmal and Muni Nathmal approached Acharya Kalugani with their discontentment.

Acharya Kalugani remonstrated that religion is a serious subject, detachment is its goal, equanimity is its *mantra* and reverence is the basis of religion. Whatever is done with self-indulgence, it is a foul. Whatever is done as per commands of a Guru is blissful, is true in religious sense. Scriptures can mislead in absence of insight; meditation turnout to be eccentric in absence of right conduct; talks of absolutism do not reach the ultimate end in the absence of saintly guidance; the worldly tendencies cannot lead to the top of universe.

It is difficult to gain true detachment without renouncing the world. One cannot look to his own faults and thinking them merits he remain unconcerned. Mighty foes like egotism cannot be destroyed by one's own indulgence. They can be easily overcome by surrendering to the teacher.

It is, therefore, dangerous in many cases to decide for yourself what is exactly suitable for you. The Guru alone can direct you to the right path. That is why spiritual knowledge has to be acquired direct from the Guru. Acharya Kalugani concluded his counsel with a couplet of Goswami Tulsidas, a popular poet of northern India. Muni Nathmal did not hear of this poet and considered him as that of Muni Tulsi and became more fearful of Muni Tulsi.

Once Muni Tulsi was not well and he stayed back. He wanted Muni Nathmal to stay with him to which Acharya Kalugani gave his consent. Muni Nathmal was cautioned by Shadhwi Jhamukuji, the Chief of Nuns, who used to check his *rajoharan* that this might debar him from, *Gurukulwas,* company of the Acharya. Muni Nathmal had a great devotion to Acharya Kalugani. He told to Acharya Kalugani what he was told by the Chief of Nuns. Acharya Kalugani sensed his deep reluctance to leave him. He touched the shoulder of Muni Nathmal and affectionately consoled him that there was no separation for them.

Muni Nathmal joined the company of Muni Tulsi happily. His service to Muni Tulsi made him more close to Muni Tulsi. His studies started again. They had heart to heart talks. Muni Tulsi lectured him that knowledge and spirituality can be acquired by pursuit with devotion and great effort. One has to struggle hard to win them. Then only things become one's own and enduring filling the mind with joy unspeakable. None can make a gift of those to another. What gained without discipline or hard labour loses its gravity, is not highly valued and does not bring happiness earned by hard struggle.

Right knowledge equip the individual with freedom from delusion and consequently equip him with true knowledge of the fundamental principles clarifying what are worthy renunciation and realization and ultimately lead to right conduct. A self-aware person will act completely within his capabilities to its pinnacle, while an ignorant person will flounder and encounter difficulty. The truly wise man will know what is right, do what is good and therefore be happy. Hence one should always be engaged in the acquisition of knowledge.

The well-meant words of Muni Tulsi stirred the mind of Muni Nathmal and an adamant resolution arose in his mind. Muni Nathmal resolved that Muni Tulsi is my sole guide in my search for the Self. My well-being absolutely rests in remaining obedient to him forever. I completely surrender myself to him by thought, word and deed. I should engage myself in the indivisible devotion to him. I would not indulge in any activity which earns his displeasure. I would not entertain any harmful thought and I would do nothing which might hurt another. I would devote myself in pursuit of right knowledge, right vision and right conduct. I would keep myself ceaselessly awakened and aware so that I would not be overtaken by *pramad,* error, or mistake, oversight, confusion, carelessness, and negligence.

Muni Nathmal got involved in achieving his aims. He was now more disciplined, full of piety and strictly adherent to his resolve. His behaviour became serious and dignified. People, however, noticed the growth of an intimate relationship between the loving, patient and forgiving teacher and his aspiring disciple. He regarded service to the Guru as a blessing and privilege. Muni Nathmal was 'marked' disciple of Muni Tulsi. Acharya Kalugani was very happy. A new pair of Mahavira-Gautam, most learned Brahmana of Vedic persuasion, who later became the main disciple of Mahavira, Plato-Aristotle, Greek philosophers, was in making.

His resolutions were building blocks of propriety of his conduct. Once he lagged behind his co-munis in his learning of lessons due to an eye-ailment, which he suffered for many weeks. He could recover the lost days of his learning through hard work and dogged perseverance.

Muni Nathmal did receive inspiration from not only his Guru but also paid heed to the advice of senior monks. Magan Muni, commonly known as Mantri Muni, had a great affection for him and was a great source of inspiration to him. He advised him that vanity and self-pride block man's progress. Man can be great only by removing these elements from his nature. A true monk is one who is not proud of his own lineage, beauty, gains and scriptural knowledge. Thus discarding all pride, he remains deeply immersed in the spiritual contemplation. Muni Nathmal pledged to be humble in his life. Even while expressing his views, he was always aware of the fact that this should not hurt the sentiments of anybody and his language should be decent.

Muni Hemraj put a lot of efforts to teach him fundamental of Jainism and made it very interesting for him, which was pretty boring and gross. He did not forget his obligation to him. He copied Sadhwi Maluji (his worldly sister and became a nun later on), who had exercised a profound influence on Nathmal's early life. She was simple and ingenuous and her heart was fathomlessly deep, long acquainted with humility, patience and sacrifice.

Muni Tulsi and Muni Nathmal again joined the company of Acharya Kalugani. In the middle of 1935 Acharya Kalugani showed the first symptoms of an ailment that later was diagnosed as boil in his palm. The illness of Acharya Kalugani showed no sign of abatement. No medication worked and the disease grew. Acharya Kalugani's suffering became almost unbearable.

Three days before the day of his ascension into the infinite, he summoned Muni Tulsi to his bedside and gave him the last instructions, almost in a whisper and declared him as his successor. The disciples stood around him. On 23rd August 1935 there was a vibration of peace and Acharya Kalugani relinquished his body and attained the ultimate ecstasy.

Acharya Kalugani had been more than his earthly mother to Muni Nathmal. His teachings and companionship still inspired him. His words rang in his ears. His solacing black eyes had been his surest refuge in his life. But he could no longer see his physical body or enjoy his seraphic smile. Muni Nathmal was stunned by this devastating event and nearing collapse. Once again it was a confrontation with the mystery of death which he witnessed in his childhood when his cousin Mahalchand died. His dormant memories awakened. He felt great desolation.

A muni should be self-contained and unemotional. Although now Acharya Tulsi was tenderer to him and he was more approachable than before. He found Acharya

Tulsi very young to shoulder the new responsibilities of an Acharya. He will not be able to give time to the studies of his disciples. These thoughts gave him grave concern.

Muni Nathmal single-mindedly concentrated on his studies and outshone other Munis and they had to admit grudgingly that Muni Nathmal was exceptionally brilliant. He studied the books in all seriousness and his mind absorbed the lesson therein and was constantly getting richer with the knowledge of books. He read the religious books of all faiths. He studied Vedanta, and *Bhagavata Gita.* He read Buddha. He delved in the Jainism and related tales. The books were his staple mental diet. He began to mature at incredibly fast rate.

His learning of scriptures was fuelling his mental growth. As Muni Nathmal grew into adolescence, a tall youth full of bloom and vigour who resembled his father, his temperament showed a marked change. His memory was prodigious. He learnt the art of grasping the essential of things, seeing truth from the widest and most comprehensive standpoint. He became keen about intellectual matters, read serious books on history, religion and literature.

Unless an individual was not given the responsibility nothing significant could be achieved. The individual could be a sharp brain or just a man of ordinary intelligence. The responsibility forced him to show some achievements. Acharya Tulsi not only encouraged him but also he took him in intellectual and religious discourses. He absorbed knowledge from living commune and personal experience. He wanted life to be kindled by life and thought kindled by thought. Acharya Tulsi felt great strength when Muni

Nathmal was with him in a gathering. This made a marked improvement in his life and an exposure of his ability to outer world.

In 1943, during World War-II, Japan bombarded Calcutta. Thousands of books stored in the Jain Mahasabha, organisation of followers of Jainism, there, were brought to Gangashahar, a suburb of Bikaner, capital of erstwhile Bikano State. Muni Nathmal got an opportunity to go through these books. He cultivated very wide reading, a passion to hear new facts and think new thought and perform fine orations. He read books in Sanskrit and Prakrit and gained proficiency in these languages.

He read dialectical materialism of Karl Marx and his principles of socialism and other teachings, Lenin, Stalin and communism in Asian and European countries and other western philosophers and became attracted to philosophy. It gave him an insight into world political system. He read Christianity and about other western religions as well as non-religion literature, heretical beliefs and atheism.

He mingled with many varying knowledge which were almost foreign to his intrinsic nature but they could not permeate and colour his character and he held to his own firmly, as was natural in a true monk. But for religions, there was an elasticity and openness in his firmness as he believed that all religions carry the same message of truth, universal sympathy, benevolence, celibacy and equanimity of mind.

Muni Nathmal read Gandhi and through him he knew John Ruskin, English critic and social theorist and Leo Tolstoy, Russian novelist, philosopher and one of the greatest writers of the world, and his sociological writings. He not only read those books but also gave deep thought as to how those branches of knowledge could be adapted for upliftment of common man.

Muni Nathmal displayed a power of clear thought, an independence of judgment and a capacity of accurate and rapid assimilation of what he has read which marked him out as possessed of higher intellectual bent and attainment. He developed unique retentive memory and displayed attention feat of *Awadhan,* concentration of memory, as and when Acharya Tulsi wished him to do so. But he discouraged it as he thought that wide publicity of his exceptional memory may hinder his *Sadhana,* Self-realization. His goal was not joy but purity and spirituality.

Muni Nathmal turned all his energy to a channel, a channel of mass awakening through literature and there was a steady stream of publications ranging from children's books to university thesis on specialized topics, from commercial publishers as well as from Jain institutions; over 200 titles can be counted, including in English.

Muni Nathmal addressed a meeting of Sanskrit scholars and gained their applause of his knowledge and grip on the language at Benaras and Poona (Kashi of south). He turned an impromptus poet of Sanskrit and a fine orator of Prakrit. A muni leads a wandering life. He exchanged ideas with people in all stations and stages of life and impressed everyone with his earnestness, eloquence, gentleness and vast knowledge. The audience was impressed and Acharya was pleased to know that he could hold his own in this new field of activity.

In the long *padyatra* undertaken by Acharya Tulsi, Muni Nathmal remained his co-walker everywhere. During these tours, while Acharya Tulsi represented the ideals of Jainism,

Muni Nathmal attracted intelligentsia and satiated its inquisitiveness regarding the moral revolution to create a new social order based on non-violence and truth.

In Muni Nathmal, there was complete surrender by obedience to his strict training. He demonstrated time and again that Acharya Tulsi is behind him in all his actions. My Guru work through me, making me his instrument, I can only bow to his will.

□

III

MUNI NATHMAL was young and full of restlessness, and had yet not the inner transformation brought about through the daily routine of a Jain monk, which requires the practice of purity, detachment and self-control. He was given every opportunity to develop his potentialities by his Guru. Over a long period of time the ideas crystallized in his mind and he was able to translate them into well defined and drafted documents.

In 1943 he wrote his first book entitled *Jiva-Ajiva,* a detailed explanation of "Pachhis Bole", universal lore. According to Jain philosophy the very basic principle of life is *Jiva,* soul, which is distinct from matter. *Jiva,* Living and *Ajiva,* Non-living, are the two realities which are responsible for the existence of the universe, which has no beginning or end in time.

A person who does not know the nature of living and the non-living substances, thus being ignorant of both, how can he know what self-control is? Jain canonical literature contains many universal laws. The book is a gist of these laws and presents a systematic and comprehensive view of the fundamental aspects of reality, relating to the basic principles. The scripture so far furnished a pastime for erudite scholars or to be enjoyed only by solitary monks became a subject of common Jain.

Most of the Jain literature was available in the vernacular. This was the first independent publication in Hindi. The book was so easy to understand that even the general reader was able to acquire its knowledge by reading it. The book became very popular. This way Muni Nathmal gained recognition amongst general public.

Acharya Tulsi kept a sharp eye on Muni Nathmal, though he appeared to give him every opportunity to release his pent-up mental energy and he wanted to use it for the *Sangh*. There was no systematic course of study for the education of the monks and nuns. Acharya Tulsi asked him to prepare a syllabus for the education of monks and nuns. Muni Nathmal carried the job very efficiently and a three tier course covering all aspects of grammar, literature, philosophy, scripture learning etc. was introduced for education of monks and nuns in the year 1946.

At the age of twenty-seven Muni Nathmal fell ill. The illness prolonged for over a month. Relief from medicines was temporary. At last he tried naturopathy. He got relief within 3 days. He recognized its importance. He started acquiring knowledge of naturopathy, complementary and alternative medicines, which emphasizes the body's innate ability to heal and maintain it. It is a holistic approach to patient care, and has its origins in ancient Indian treatment and was prevalent in Jain monks of yore, when cures were effected rather by regulating diet than by the use of medicines. Various diseases were diagnosed by observation, by touching and taking the changes in the rate, rhythm and force of the pulse.

Jain scholars devised a system of time based on breaths

and beating of pulse. They still use *ghadi, muhurta* and *pahar* of this system in their rituals as measurement of time.

Muni Nathmal read Luis Pune. He read western theory of fasting vis-à-vis *vrats* prescribed in Jainism. He read Ayurveda and other branches of cure. He read human anatomy and respiration system. He experimented with food and food related habits, sound healing art (recitation of some auspicious words or *mantras*).

To improve the mind without the cultivation of physical body is a hollow victory. Spirituality and health go side by side. He has given us many books on health and spirituality. Eating and breathing are the main innate faculties of the body. It is more important that how we eat than what we eat though it is also. He established the prominence of small topics ignored by modern man like proper chewing of food, developing taste of individual item of food, serene countenance at the time of taking food and even unless cooking is performed with a pure mind and concentration, the food is not palatable. A new definition of balanced diet has been coined by him.

Jainism combines health consciousness along with rituals. According to Jain tradition, among the 12 types of penances, the first four – *anashan* (fasting), *unodari and atheism* (eating less than what hunger demands), *vritti-sankshepa* (selective eating) and *rasa-parityaga* (taste-selection) – are particularly good for health. Mahavira did not neglect the body. Mahavira said that you hold infinite potential within the fortress of your mind and body.

Mahavira was meticulous about diet. Mahavira immediately after 12 years of spiritual dedication, when he became all-knowing — past, present and future — observed fast for six months (All the penances of Mahavira were without water. He did not drink water for more than four or six months even at a stretch.) and one of the prerequisites of his 13 point vow was that he would break the fast only on getting boiled cereal in alms.

The simplest food and the least amount of it that will keep body and soul together, combined with abstinence from fleshly, earthly pleasure will eventually lead to spiritual perfection. He gave two important words about diet – *Hitchar* (helpful), and *Mitchar* (lesser in quantity). Muni Nathmal added a new word, *Ritchar* (earned), in this definition. He turned his attention to research into mind and mental health. He became interested in meditation and *yoga*.

The study gave Muni Nathmal a host of stimulating ideas. As a result of the long struggle, countless sacrifices and martyrdoms, the country gained freedom from the British rule on 15th August, 1947. Nation building was the slogan of free India. Muni Nathmal had acquired knowledge of all subjects and on the strength of knowledge his attention went to social evils, irrational customs and blind faiths such as castes, backwardness in women, such as child marriage, forced marriage of unequal in health, age and intelligence and endless superstitions and ignorance, plaguing the society. It was a turn of mass awakening.

Muni Nathmal wrote a book *Ankhen Kholo*. It was an attack on ignorance born out of illiteracy aggravated by social evils and orthodox mindset. There was a lot of fuss but it had a revolutionary effect on ladies and girls. He had the support of his Guru, Acharya Tulsi. He had taken his permission before the book was sent to press. Acharya Tulsi in his daily sermon took these topics one by one and this way the duo, Guru and disciple, started teaching the masses.

The *Nayamod* movement for eradicating the social evils prevalent in many regions of Rajasthan was vigorous and fruitful step undertaken by both Acharya Tulsi and Muni Nathmal. As a result of this campaign, centuries old evil traditions of keeping *purdah* (veil) over the face of womenfolk, keeping widows in seclusion for 12 months making her almost hunch-backed and the contempt prevalent against them, as also the unnecessary expenditures on the occasion of death of parents, etc. were all brought to an end.

Freedom was the hope and aspiration of millions of India's people toiling in their brown fields under the scorching tropical sun. The wandering monk, who heard the piteous moans of the teeming millions, had an understanding of India.

In 1948, when the political leaders were busy in framing the Constitution of free India, Muni Nathmal gave a deep thought and a deliberation to the fate of the poor country vis-à-vis oligarchic republics presided by an elected king for a specific period of yore when the glory of India was at a zenith, the period of vigorous prosperity of formidable Chandragupta Maurya, known as Sandrocottes, to the western world, who in his youth had met Alexander the Great and defeated his General, Seleucus and receiving Kandhar in gift by his retreating army. At an older age, Chandragupta renounced his throne and material possessions to join a wandering group of Jain monks. He spent the last twelve years of his life as a Jain monk, seeking self-realization. Chandragupta was a disciple of Jain Scholar Bhadrabahu and he observed the rigorous but self purifying Jain ritual of *Santhara,* fast unto death, in a rock cave at Sravanelagola, Karnataka.

Thereafter, Samprati, the grandson of Ashoka also embraced Jainism. The kings followed the teachings of Mahavira. The slackness in subsequent generation was the reason of their downfall; and conquest by Turks and Europeans.

Muni Nathmal also analyzed histories of various countries and their philosophical and political systems, the European civilization and materialistic development of the West, which they achieved with common co-operation and united efforts and sharing by all without distinction of caste and creed.

The teachings of Mahavira are radical and continue to be relevant even today. As the scientific tenor is developed further, its relevance will be appreciated more. For regeneration of India, selfishness, jealousy, greed and lust of power should be kept away and they must dedicate themselves to the service of the poor, illiterate, the hungry and sick. His new book was *Vishwa Ki Sthtiti* published in 1948.

Following the British conquest of the country, English education was introduced in the country. Western science, history and philosophy were studied in the Indian colleges and universities. The use of standard language is often a mark of polite behaviour; good grammar and approved pronunciation mark a man as cultivated.

The educated youths, allured by the glamour, began to

mould their thoughts according to this new light. The intellectual and aggressive European culture had a suppressing effect on the glorious heritage of the indigenous civilization. To retrace young minds, unwilling to accept spiritual truth without rational proof, by acquiring wrong information of truth and reality and to put them on the path of right knowledge and action, the necessity of equally forceful modern Indian language was the need of time.

Hindi, with its roots in Sanskrita, dear to *pandits'* hearts, was the chief vernacular of the Aryavrata, Northern India, the sacred land of Aryans where the Hindu culture had originated. It is a complete language in the sense that it has its own scripts, pronunciation and grammar but for its vocabulary, we are stuck with it. It could not develop words commensurate with the development of different branches of knowledge, which was a great hindrance in its getting an all-India acceptance. It was influenced by Vedanta and words of Buddhism have also been assimilated, but Jainism remained untouched.

Jainism is not merely a reform of the orthodox religion, but an altogether separate religious system, quite distinct and independent from other systems, but, of course, it is an aspect of Indian life, culture and philosophy. Jainism is a specific trend of thought distinct from Hindusim and Buddhism. Jains have their own scripture and it is one of the eight major faiths of the world.

Jainism is an important constituent of composite and civilization and heritage of India. Jains, though few in number, have enriched the religious and cultural life of India far more than their small numbers would suggest. Their temples are the most exquisite and architecturally sophisticated of any ever built in India.

Mahavira regarded all men and women equal and did not stratify human being on the basis of caste and creed. Not only that, he said, "Even a *Chandala*, dog-eater (the outcaste), should be respected and counted as a *devata* if he is endowed with Right Belief". He gave equal importance to ladies.

Mahavira made religion simple and natural, free from elaborate ritual complexities. His attempt is that man should try to learn to distinguish between essentials and non-essentials. He opposed all sorts of discrimination and snobbery and felt the significance of his teachings for the average man struggling with life's problems. The common man, ignorant of the scriptures was brought in the light of truth.

Mahavira preached to them in the language they were accustomed to understand and used comparisons and analogies to make his point clear in suitable situations. Questions are the most effective method of eliciting knowledge and his answers to the questions of his disciples are the basis of his teachings.

Not only people of various religions, faiths, views and age had the liberty to attend but also birds and animals too had a free access to his sermons. In an era when it was impossible to think of equality between man and man, Mahavira declared that all things are equally vast and independent. Translating his declaration into deeds, he admitted men and women of all castes and creed impartially in his fourfold *Sangh*, religious organization.

Agams have explained their adaptability and their quality of being understood simultaneously by all the living beings present at his discourse. The most of that literature called Prakrit is devoted to Jainism. This language is a master piece of brevity and substantive expression. Its naturally born words make it very simple and lucid.

Jain literature is remarkable for its variety and vastness and chronological sequence of events, not merely confined to religious tradition, but also to other branches such as heaven and hell, stars and planets, history, geography, conception and evolution of life, molecular theory, atomic physics and other advanced scientific topics, politics, sociology, trade and commerce. Muni Nathmal engaged in research and publication of Jain literature was handicapped to make this knowledge of scholars available to public at large.

Words are the symbols of knowledge; the keys to accurate thinking. He gave deep thought to the problem and wrote a book titled, *Hindi Jan-Jan Ki Bhasha*. He emphasized the importance of language. He gave many suggestions as to how Hindi can enrich its vocabulary as well as by accepting popular words or words which have no substitutes in Hindi from other languages such as Bengali, Tamil, Kannada, Gujarati etc. so that Hindi can gain a respectable position.

The wide popularity and acceptance of Jain faith and philosophy is the Jain *shraman,* saints and hermits, and the rich heritage of treasures of knowledge left behind by the holy saints or *Acharyas*. Literature is like a vast ocean of knowledge and the credit for its protection, patronage, preservation, nurturing, reprography and documentation goes to revered and learned saints and hermits who took upon themselves this onerous responsibility from time to time.

The pious institution was besieged with two major problems. Some misguided zealots wanted to take legal cover to ban or attack this pious institution on grounds of beggary, ignoring the high calibre of Jain monks who lives for ever in the hearts and minds of millions of people for whose mental, emotional and spiritual upliftment they work all through their lives. They hail from devout family of respectable status and undergo a rigorous procedure before they are initiated and it cannot be said initiation by force of adverse circumstances or by an accidental rise of the spirit of intense non-attachment by distressing events.

The antiquity of institution did not have any meaning for them. They also wanted that monkhood to those who did not reach adulthood should also be banned. Muni Nathmal has given very appropriate answer to them in his two books on *Bhikshavriti* and *Bal Dikshaw Par Ek Manovagyanik Drishtikon* for the purpose of creating awakening.

Mahavira systemized pre-existing Jain doctrines, and organized *Jain Sangh,* communion of monks, nuns, *shravak-shravikas,* listeners and lay followers of true faith. He laid down rules and prescribed the definite *vrats,* vows, rules of conduct, to be observed by its followers. All these rules of conduct are directed towards the main aim of achieving freedom of the soul from the *karmic* matter, i.e., attaining liberation. The rules of conduct have been so designed that all persons would be in a position to follow them.

A vow is a solemn resolve made after deliberation to observe a particular rule of conduct; it is made before a saint on his advice or voluntarily to protect oneself against possible lapses of conduct. The object is to control the mind and mould one's conduct along the spiritual path.

A vow affords stability to the will and guards its votary from the evils of temptation or of unguarded life; it gives purpose to life and healthy direction to our thoughts and actions. It helps the growth of self control and protects against the pitfalls of free life. The vows are such as are intended to protect the society from harm by projecting oneself on the righteous path.

Jain monks practise non-violence up to the hilt. The Five *Mahavrata* are termed root-virtues, because in their absence other saintly virtues cannot be acquired. It is evident that the rules of conduct and the austerities, which ascetic has to observe, are of an extremely difficult character and that only a person who is possessed of right knowledge of soul and matter in all their aspects and is prepared for a life of penance and austerities can become ascetic. An ascetic has the sole aim of pursuing the spiritual path is in full control of his senses and in a position to curb his passions quite easily due to his religious learning and spiritual discipline can observe the vows fully .

The whole system of ascetic morality is worked out most minutely. The entire spiritual career of the soul is divided into 14 *gunasthan,* stages and levels of merit, which determine where exactly the person stands in his inner development. The soul marches from bondage and gross ignorance to final liberation and omniscience, gradually overpowering at different stages divided into eleven *pratima,* steps.

These eleven steps include observance of the five precepts as well as practice of self-contemplation three times a day with a view to obtaining mental equipoise, observance of weekly fasts, abstaining from taking green vegetables as also taking food before sunrise and after sunset; ceasing to take interest in worldly matters, and so on. When he reaches the eleventh stage, he is fully prepared to follow the severe course of ascetic life. In all stages up to the eleventh, regress may take place, and the soul may even fall back to the first stage. When he reaches the twelfth, however, the passion, etc. are destroyed, and he begins meditation. When all *karma* is destroyed, the soul attains its fullest spiritual status.

A *shravak* listens to and accordingly follows religious precepts. The precepts work as an inspiration for acquisition of right type of daily life. A *shravak* has to look after his family and adjust himself to the social and political conditions in which he lives and would find it very difficult to live up to such ideals because of its uncompromising emphasis on austerity and self-purification. Good conduct and self-realization is equally important for persons living in worldly life and they should be just and honest in earning their living and collection of wealth.

Mahavira prescribed 12 vows, 11 meditations and 3 aspirations for *shravaks*. They should bear the 21 virtues and enumerated 15 characteristics a *shravak* should develop: he should not be haughty; he should be humble; should not be unsteady but steady; should not be deceitful but simple and straight; not probing but grave; he should not shun others; he should not entertain anger for a long time; he should think well of his friends; he should not grow arrogant after receiving knowledge; he should not publicize the shortcomings of others; he should not be angry with his friends; he should speak well even of unlikable friends in their absence; he should not indulge in violent quarrels; he should be wise; he should be of noble descent; he should be bashful and of steady mind.

Acharya Tulsi felt the need of minimum moral code at every station and stage of life. He wanted to modify/simplify these rules in the context of present life-style under the current political system. Muni Nathmal gave his word to obey his Acharya's wish. Muni Nathmal compiled a code of right conduct in the form of simple Do's and Don'ts rules of everyday life for householders and housewives, for students etc.

Muni Nathmal conceived the philosophical background of those codes of conduct and assisted his guru in planning all its activities. Acharya Tulsi was much impressed and gave it a shape of "Anuvrat Movement", a peace movement based on small vows, with an objective to establish self-control, friendship, peace, morality and a society free of exploitation, and freeing people from drug addiction and other vices in the year 1949. Muni Nathmal wrote many books on its philosophy, working and rules.

The message of Jina is carried by the Acharyas. The responsibility of the spiritual well being of the entire Jain *Sangh*, comunity- hermits and lay followers, rests on the shoulders of the Acharya. Before reaching that state of Acharya, one has to do an in-depth study and gain mastery over the *Agama*. In addition to acquiring a high level of spiritual excellence, they also have the ability to lead the monastic communion, know various languages of the country and sound knowledge of other philosophies, ideologies and religions of the region and of the world.

The best methodology of teaching is to cultivate

politeness in conduct and behaviour, others will be automatically inspired. According to *Uttradhyan Sutra,* canonical treatise, only he can pioneer others on the path of politeness, who has himself become conscious of the need to be polite, free from desires, and who has developed good conduct in himself. A candle lights other candles. It never preaches but it simply lights other candles and thereby inspires others. The Acharyas are like candles and they light hundreds of candles. So they have to remain enlightened to keep enlightening others. The Acharya has to be highly disciplined, more cautious and more awakened and practice greater restraint than others.

Acharya Tulsi showed early leadership qualities since his school time. He took his monk's vows at the age of 11 with remarkable dedication, and by the time he was 16, he had already started attracting acolytes. This young talent through his dynamism and sense of purpose captured the attention of Kalugani who nominated him to be his successor when he was just 22 years old. That was the rare incident in Jain history that a 22 year youth has been given the responsibility to lead senior and learned sages. He surpassed all estimates. He transformed the Terapanth.

Acharya Tulsi was a great visionary and conceived many innovative programmes and schemes to uplift the mental, moral and emotional status of his disciples and followers. He had the unique quality to translate his vision into actual practice. He initiated the highest number of monks/nuns. He has been an accomplished poet, an author as well as a distinguished religious leader. He broke all records in barefoot marches and travelled to almost every part of India. He showed particular concern for education and preaching, putting emphasis on study, research and writing by monks, and by nuns as well.

The Anuvrat Movement which he initiated in 1949 works for moral uplift, honesty and a non-violent, non-exploitive society. He was a proponent of Jain unity regardless of sectarian differences. There are many monks known for their scholarship, prepared by Acharya Tulsi. Muni Nathmal is one of them.

Acharya Tulsi was softer than the flower, where kindness was concerned and stronger than the thunder, where principles were at stake. He commanded respect and obedience by his character and to live near him demanded of the disciples' purity of thought and concentration of mind. The outer world saw only the struggles and restlessness of his wandering, but not the inner transformation brought about through the practice of purity, detachment, self control and meditation.

Muni Nathmal has seen Acharya Tulsi from very close and gives the credit of making him a true monk. In 1952 in the first biography of his Guru, *Acharya Tulsi - Jiwan Par Ek Drishti,* he paid a most touching tribute to his Guru. Muni Nathmal has written many books on his Guru every time when he scaled new heights. He has taken the Jainism to the new heights.

Acharya Tulsi was one of the great Acharyas and reformers, who opened the door of world wide publicity to Jainism and Muni Nathmal played a very major role in it. Muni Nathmal has expressed his love, reverence, devotion and dedication to his Guru in his many books on his personality, teachings, his creations, and almost in every speech and publication.

Acharya Bhikshu was the first of the Terapanth ascetics. The various beliefs and teachings of the religious orders of those times greatly influenced his thinking and he chose to follow the way of the search for truth and to understand it. Acharya Bhikshu studied and analyzed the teachings of Mahavira thoroughly and on this basis he compiled his own ideologies and principles of the Jain way of life. Based on the doctrines he propagated, Acharya Bhikshu rigorously followed the principles and thus set an example for all to follow. He showed the way for the life of discipline, purity and self-control.

Acharya Bhikshu was an innovative visionary. He established new dimensions of religion and a demarcation between social obligation and liberation of soul. He advanced theory of purity in the means of production to prevent misuse of resources. He gave meritorious forethought to non-violence, kindness and benevolence. In pursuit of this objective he sacrificed material goals, honour and luxuries. By adhering strictly to the doctrines he laid down, he overcame the weaknesses of the body and human character and led the way of a celestial life.

Acharya Bhikshu revolutionized the various principles which had become meaningless with the passing of time and gave conception and birth to those tenements. He visualized a systematic, well established and orderly religious sect and saw it taking shape through 'Terapanth'. To organize and stabilize this religious order he propagated the ideology of one Acharya, one principle, one thought and similar thinking became the ideal for other religious sects. Acharya Bhikshu was an ideal of tolerance, non-violence, generosity and equality and at every instance of his life he strived to stand against what was immoral and wrong in society fearlessly. The life of Acharya Bhikshu sets out an example for human to follow a life of the positive human traits.

The life of Acharya Bhikshu was a prodigy of ups and downs that tested and moulded him to become a supreme individual. While the first half of the life of Acharya Bhikshu is related to how he faced ordeals and difficulties, the second half reveals (unfolds) the success and accomplishments. It is this narration of the life and times of Acharya Bhikshu which has been compiled and presented in the *Acharya Bhikshu Vichar and Darshan* by Muni Nathmal.

Science as we know it today was unknown to antiquity. Instead there existed knowledge with philosophical and mystical truths, which was highly developed in India. Jain thinkers gave elaborate thought to the realm of life and death and found a self-sustaining mechanism of systematic operation of total deterministic control over destinies, which operates endogenously as natural universal law.

Millennia before modern science proved the existence of molecules (1906) and atoms (1920) Jain scholars had postulated the existence of *karmic* matter as extremely subtle and microscopic particles that cannot be perceived by senses or measurements and Doctrine of *Karma,* which is in consonance with the law of causality of physics, as cause and effect mechanism of human predicament. Anyone who would have suggested that these "indivisible" particles were made up of even subtler units like quarks and leptons only a hundred years ago may have been dismissed, though such theories were in existence.

Jain seers comprehended subtle truth with the help of

subtle consciousness and could foresee what science discovered much later on. Their philosophy is based on the foundations of experience and direct perception. It will take physicists some time to explain it.

Jainism is a system of laws, but natural rather than moral laws. There is an innate moral order to the cosmos, self-regulating through the workings of *karma*. Morality and ethics are important not because of a god, but because a life that is led in agreement with moral and ethical principles is considered beneficial. In fact, it forms a central and fundamental part of Jain faith and is intricately connected to other concepts like *ahimsa,* non-violence, *aparigraha,* non-possession and *anekantvada,* multiplicity of view points.

Jainism conveys a different meaning than is commonly understood in the Hindu philosophy and western civilization. It attaches responsibility to the individual action and eliminates existence of divine grace or retribution. Every person or every entity is a creator of self destiny and influx, bondage, stoppage, and shedding of *karmas* and salvation are solely functions of the soul. God has no role to play in Jainism as a dispenser of *karmas*.

The doctrine of *karma* provides a rational and satisfying explanation to the apparently inexplicable universal chain of causation. It states that fate is nothing except the result of past good and evil deeds, the way of performing those deeds and the intention working behind that action. Its intensity varies with level of intention. So it can be said to some extent that luck is pre-recorded by the past deeds. But it should not be understood that nothing can be done in present to overcome negative past for creating bright future. What one has done, one can undo. Jainism truly believes that action is the manager of luck and the present is more powerful than the past and future. Doctrine of *karma* suggests awareness of our actions so that we can grow and change in positive ways. So, whatever be the movement of *karma,* it does not stand against industrious perseverance.

Karmic matter is actually the agent that enables consciousness to act within the material context of the universe. When attracted to our consciousness, they are stored in our interactive *karmic* field i.e. *karmic* body. Thus the *karmas* are the subtle matter surrounding the consciousness of the soul. When these two components, i.e., consciousness and *karma* interact, we experience the life as we know it at present. Soul or consciousness is formless and invisible, and it is everywhere in the body. *Aajiva* portions are divided into three bodies: physical or gross body, *Tejas,* luminous body or body of vital energy, subtle body and *Karmic* body, micro subtle body.

The *Physical* body is the material body of the living being that is obtained from the mother's womb. It is a companion of one life and subject of science and has been studied in great deal A person cannot be liberated without the help of this body. Hence it is the most important body of the human being. At the time of death, the soul leaves this body behind. There are other bodies which are composed of invisible matter.

The *Tejas* body supports and provides control on the physical body and manages the system. It discharges the functions with the help of vital energy, *prana. Tejas* body receives *prana* through breathing and obstruction in the inflow of *prana,* energy stops functioning of the body system resulting in death. At the time of death, it accompanies the soul and helps to create the next material body for the soul.

The *Karma* body is the subtlest and invisible. It is the base of all the other bodies, gross as well as subtle. The *Tejas* and gross bodies cannot exist without the *Karma* body. The soul is released from the gross body when the latter dies, but not from the *Karma* body. Even when the soul leaves it, it comes up again before the soul. It cannot be relinquished easily.

This body is composed of dispositions, predilections and traces left by past desires and it is difficult to get rid of it. This is the real prison and due to our mind, speech and behaviour, increases or decreases continuously. It has tremendous memory capacity and it, in fact, contains information and intelligence that control all functions of mind and body. At the time of death, the soul is accompanied by this body for the next birth and along with *Tejas* body forms the basis of the other newly produced physical body. It also provides the fruits of living being's past action when due.

The *karma* body and the *tejas* body never depart and both of them are always in union with the soul. This union is maintained till the soul attains the state of emancipation. The liberation of the soul is, in fact, getting freedom from the imprisonment by these two bodies. Both these bodies are inactive, whereas soul is active.

Since ages Jains have produced abundant of doctrinal material dealing with the *karmic* mechanism, causes of *karmas*, types of *karmas*, nature and duration of *karmas*, liberation from *karmas* and the like. Muni Nathmal read eastern and western philosophy. He was a contemporary thinker of Jain philosophy and continued to solve the riddles of abstruse fundamentals of the scriptures in a popular language and profoundly contributed Jain literature. He discussed this theory elaborately in his book *Karmavad*.

Everything in the universe seems to be just a vibration. Every elementary particle, even our thoughts and consciousness are just vibrations. The soul vibrates under the influence of conscious activity such as thinking, creativity, intentions, sense of humour and emotions. The soul is completely surrounded by the *karma* body and the vibrations have to pass through it. In this process the vibrations are coloured by the *karma* present in the *karma* body and acquires the characteristics of the *karma* which are acting at that instant.

From there these waves enter the *tejas* body and on interaction with the *tejas* body are transformed into a kind of perceptible subtle physical force which forms the basis of one's inner feeling. It is called *Lesya,* colour of passion or psychic colour. Some of the waves bypass the *tejas* body and directly enter the brain in the physical body, and mature into the physical imprint of all our past memories and impressions.

The characteristics originate from *karma* and manifest in the physical brain and the mind works accordingly. The hypothalamus, a part of the brain, receives these vibrations and transforms them into emotions. The mind does not have any concrete existence of its own or function by itself. The flow of emotions begins and turns on the mind.

The *lesyas* produce feelings which interact with the

endocrine glands and influence the secretion of hormones. The hormones mix with the blood and reach the nervous system and the brain which manage and control our emotions, thoughts, speech, conduct and behaviour. Thus the *karma* acting through *lesya* and hormones determine our personality and traits. The endocrine glands provide a transformer that establishes connection between the subtle body and the physical system. These glands thus convert the signals of the soul into chemicals which finally control the body and mind.

Our thoughts are based on our feelings and emotions and do not have independent existence. Thoughts rise and subside with feelings. We can exercise control on our body, mind and speech but the feelings are beyond our control. The feeling, in fact, need purification and refinement, once purified there will be no need of control.

The effect of thinking, of the environment, and of food falls on the body and the mind either deeply or lightly. Whole universe vibrates and rays radiating from cosmic bodies have also its impact. *Lesya* acts as a liaison between the soul and the physical body. They work in both directions. They pick up the signals from the soul and produce feelings and through it transmit the message to the mind and body. On the other hand whatever is performed by mind, speech and body is communicated by *lesya* to the *Karma* body. Thus the entire communication between the subtle body and the physical body is through *lesya*.

The *lesyas* are of two kinds – *bhava* (pysical) *lesya* and *dravya* (physical) *lesya*. The *bhava lesya* is connected with the soul (the flow of emotions) and the physical *lesya,* which is also called aura or ethereal body, is a formation of radiating material atoms. It is an envelope of light. Its dimness or brightness depends upon the psysical *lesya*.

All that is material has colour, odour, taste and tactility. Colour is the object of the eye, the organ of seeing. In the acquisition of sensory knowledge, the eye is our most vivid sense organ. The senses of taste, touch etc. also provide direct knowledge, still in everyday living, the knowledge that comes with seeing is generally regarded as the most direct and tangible.

The physical *lesyas* in the form of waves have colours and are classified on that basis. There are six main kinds of *lesya*:

Krishna Lesya — Colour is dull blackish,
Neel Lesya — Colour is dark blue,
Kapot Lesya —It has pigeon like colour,
Tejo Lesya — Colour is bright red.
Padma Lesya - Colour is bright yellow,
Shukla Lesya - whitish bright colour.

Each kind of *lesya* represents some specific qualities in a person. The first three types are the malevolent *lesyas* and indicate negative qualities. The last three types are benevolent *lesyas* indicating positive qualities in a person. A person can have different *lesya* at different times depending on his current *bhava* but only one *lesya* is present at any time.

The *lesya* is the mental disposition or innermost feeling which one assumes under a given set of circumstances as well as disposition itself and is closely related to the Jain theory of *Karma* and has also found recognition in other systems of knowledge.

The Doctrine of *Lesya* is very comprehensive and of far reaching influence. Awakening and activation of *lesya*, its sensation, impact of *lesya* on mind and body, purification of lesya, upgradation of *lesya*, its application for development of mental, verbal and physical stability, and from the point of view of both personality and spiritual development, the field of *lesya* is very extensive and elaborated in *Uttardhyan* and other *Agama* so much so that it occupies a quarter of its space. Muni Nathmal, who has written many books on development of human personality, man's place in universe and his duties to himself and fellow creatures, has dwelt on this subject in his book *Abhanmandal*.

In the year 1954, Acharya Tulsi came to know that *Pitakas*, sacred canons of Buddhism, are being edited. He asked Muni Nathmal if it could be done for *Agama*. The task was as forbidding as it was complex and difficult.

Nothing seemed impossible to Muni Nathmal against the wish of his Guru. No time was lost by him to take up the job in hand. He pursued research with openness, honesty and dedication to bring forth the revelations and incarnated the whole era of Mahavira. He shared his knowledge with others as he progressed and kept on reviewing the subtleness and broad scope of Jain philosophy. He concurrently wrote many books on Jain philosophy, logic, deep logic (adoration verse), and history etc., in the light of his newly acquired knowledge of scriptures.

Initially, the inexperienced team of monks and nuns headed by Muni Nathmal interpreting, investigating and analyzing the *Agama*, fixed a target of 5 years. It was a very difficult task. The words, which were in vogue 2,500 years ago, had lost their identity. To know its real impact seemed impossible. Muni Nathmal who had blessings and direction of his Guru could do the job with his great mental prowess. The transcription ran into over a hundred thousand pages spread over 32 volumes. They realized that a period of 50 years was not enough as every interpretation gave a new dimension of knowledge.

Muni Nathmal started to see through the eyes of the *Agama*. He started visualizing how the rich knowledge of Mahavira and subsequent Acharyas could benefit the mankind. This knowledge, if propagated properly, could be a great boon for the mankind. He thought of further research into canonical treaties, which was not possible for any wandering individual or a group. It needed a mammoth organization. He conceived of an education centre to further these studies.

Muni Nathmal masterminded the conception and opened his mind to Acharya Tulsi. This gave birth to Jain Vishva Bharati University under the spiritual patronship of Acharya Tulsi in an area of 1,00,600 sq meters, 380 kilometres west of New Delhi at Ladnun, the birth place of his Guru but a place far from bustling cities, with an objective to revive the truths and values hidden in the ancient Indian traditions in general and Jain traditions in particular, through the activities of teaching, research, spiritual meditation, publications, service, cultural values and synthesis. The university is, however, free from any religious affiliations.

The Jain Vishva Bharati University is an endeavour in the direction of putting into practice and to promote and propagate the high ideals of non-violence, non-absolutist outlook, tolerance and peaceful co-existence for the welfare of mankind. The institution combines theoretical with practical research, i.e., knowledge and meditation. It draws its spiritual strength and direction from the Acharya, who is above any sectarian bias.

The publication of *Agamic* literature was started under the supervision of Muni Nathmal as the Chief Editor, Translator and Commentator. Muni Nathmal was the main source of inspiration for all academic and research activities conducted there. The university started several innovative courses to bring about a revolutionary change in the field of education. Post-graduate courses as well as research facilities are provided in the subjects of non-violence and peace, social work, Jainology and comparative religion, philosophy, and Prakrit.

Yoga is a popular subject. It has good name in the western world and is in great demand among the educated class. In 1959, Acharya Tulsi visited Calcutta. Shanti Prasad Jain, proprietor of *Times of India,* an industrialist and a very learned Jain scholar, a rare combination, was a frequent visitor to Acharya Tulsi and member of his entourage and was highly impressed by the deep knowledge and critical analysis of various matters of Muni Nathmal. He informed that his overseas friends wanted to know if Jains had any system of *Yoga.*

Yoga and spirituality were long cherished subject of Muni Nathmal. Mention of meditation techniques is available in Jain scriptures that have been forgotten with time. Such incidents asked him to retrieve what had been lost in the dark ages. Acharya Tulsi wished and spiritual religious research became his main focus.

Jainism is known for its principle of non-violence. It is a religion in which all life is considered worthy of respect and it emphasizes equality of all life, advocating the protection of even the smallest creatures. A major characteristic of Jain belief is the emphasis on the consequences of not only physical but also mental behaviour. Jains believe that all living beings possess a soul, and therefore, great care and awareness is required in going about one's business in the world.

Mahavira said, *"Padhamam nanam tao daya"*. First awareness, then compassion. Even compassion delivered out of ignorance is not helpful in freedom from bondage, so first awareness then compassion. Eternal vigilance is necessary to annihilate the powerful enemy—lust. *Apramada,* ceaseless awareness and awakening, is the basis of Mahavira's *sadhana,* dedicated spiritual practice, which is not a process but sheer spiritual consciousness—a pure awareness. It is a sustained endeavour to cleanse the mind of unwholesome mental forces which run beneath the stream of consciousness vitiating our thinking, values, attitudes and actions.

No matter what one does, it is always there. In fact, it is perfectly consonant with all that one does. It has an enlivening and refreshing effect. Whatever is undertaken with spiritual concentration becomes highly efficacious. Real *Apramada* is, or should be, a state of effortless spiritual awareness, not one that comes as a laboured accomplishment.

Mahavira did not separate *Apramada* from any human activity. Spiritual concentration has to be trained on anything and everything it has to coincide with the flow of life, with the ongoing activity, with all undertakings. Viewed thus, spirituality is co-extensive and interchangeable with life. Elimination of *Moorchha,* delusion, and eschewal of *Pramada,* indolence, opens the gateway to a pure life.

Yoga, in general term, is a system of exercises for body and for controlling of breathing, used by people who want to become fitter or to relax. It is a control of the fluctuations of the mind stuff and consists of body discipline, mental control and meditating in the belief that one can become united with the spirit of the universe in this way. The goal of every *yogi* is achievement of a state called *samadhi,* release.

Jainism is basically *atman,* soul-oriented, religion. The *atman* is both bondage of *karma* and a source of liberation. The law of *karma* occupies the same supreme place as God occupies elsewhere as main moving force. The individual has to nullify the bondage of *karma* to achieve *moksha.* Mild, moderate and intense — an appropriate system of meditation on each of these three levels has been prescribed in Jainism. All these techniques primarily refer to *karma* not to the body.

The system of Jain meditation is a process of demolishing the *karmu* and dissolving thc past impressions. Only the purity of emotion and not its goodness or evil may free the soul from all bondage of *karma,* which is complete deliverance. Even in *punya,* good deed, there is a throbbing attraction within us and we attract *karma* particles. With desire it leads to becoming a *deva,* demigod, or to the sovereignty of *deva, asuras* and men, but not to liberation. But the right conduct which is *vitrag,* free from desires, that, and that alone, will lead to final liberation.

In Jainism fourteen *gunsthan,* stages of progress of soul

due to development of its qualities are indicated through which the soul progresses from impure matter on to final liberation. *Gunsthans* describe the path, modalities and pre-requisites for the bonded soul to become liberated soul through the path of internal progress.

Yoga in Jainism is a systematic combination of different physical and mental exercises done with the purpose of fleeing the soul from everything that is material. *Yoga* has been developed in accordance with Jain metaphysical attitude and consists of introspection; reflection, meditation, equanimity and all that stop the inflow of *karmas*.

Jainism is a lifestyle of *samyam,* self-control and *sanwar,* eradication of worldly tendencies, to achieve genuine freedom. Self-control cannot be achieved without purification of body and mind.

In Jain tradition twelve kinds of purification is very important in the context of meditation. Fasting, control over diet, undertaking of various pledges, and complete abstention from rich heavy foods—all these four elements are extremely important from the point of view of body-purification.

Next is posture and control of the mind and the senses. After achieving control over the senses and the passions, a method of purification of the mental flaws has been laid down. At this level, it is necessary to affect the dissolution of the ego and total surrender. In order to develop knowledge-consciousness, the mendicant takes to studies. Then only the groundwork is laid for the practice of meditation. Meditation undertaken without first passing through the requisite stages cannot be continued for long.

The consummation of meditation is renunciation, complete detachment.

Meditation was an integral part of Mahavira life. Meditation and *Kayosagga,* deep relaxation, had been his tools for self-purification. As soon as he initiated into monkhood he practised *kayosagga* and meditation and observed fast for three days. He felt that meditation was very important although fasting was no less. For meditation it was essential for the body to be in a perfect condition. Such perfection was possible only through fasting or controlled eating. Fasting prepares the necessary background for meditation. To be able to practice meditation it is necessary to purify mental and physical background.

Mahavira, during the period of 12 years of his spiritual meditation, concentrated on his inner-self or soul purification standing or squatting with his eyes fixed on the tip of nose, a disposition which makes possible intuitions that transcends consciousness. He turned to stone and nothing could distract him any more. *Kewal Jnan,* absolute knowledge, dawned on him through insight born out of meditation and contemplation and beyond the limitation of senses. Mahavira and thereafter some Jain saints had also practised it, but this mode of contemplation gradually disappeared.

Muni Nathmal continued his search for fact finding. Jain scholars in the past worked on the subject of meditation. He read *Yoga* treatise of Hemchandra Suri, Acharya Yashovijay, who worked on *yoga* in Jainism, Hari Bhadar Suri, the most significant knowledgeable person of Jain *yoga,* who based metaphysical theory of Jainism of spiritual achievement to destroy *karma* and to achieve salvation on steps as eight organs of *Yoga of Patanjali.*

Muni Nathmal read *Patanjali,* ancient exponent of *Yoga, Gherand Samhita,* a manual of *yoga.* He attended *yoga* camp run by *Vipasana,* a system of yoga available in Buddhism. Jainism and Buddhism are branches of ascetic culture. *Vipasana* was not a new word for him. It has also mention in *agamas.* He was a scholar of contemporary philosophy and studied human nature deeply and had his own conclusion.

Muni Nathmal had a powerful urge to learn. Day in and day out he kept learning and growing intellectually by a serious and extensive study of *Acharang Sutra,* canonical treatise on meditation, arranging the fact in a systematic and chronological way, identifying a procedure to measure them on scientific scale, experimentation and experience. He shared his knowledge at every stage. He wrote concurrently many books, *Jain Yoga, Manoyoga, Chetana Ka Udhwarhoyan, Mahavir Ki Sadhana Ka Rahasya.* Things started getting crystal clear to him.

Muni Nathmal could trace the seeds of a non-assertive and pliable system of *Dharamdhyan,* meditation, as practised by Jain scholars in the past and scattered in Agama, which he did not see anywhere else. He felt the need to organise that knowledge to perfect a complete system of meditation.

Muni Nathmal continued his research, discourses and debates, and started masterminding the subject. He did his experiments for days together. Firstly he did in lonely places and subsequently in places surrounded by others. He did it at different times of the day. He concentrated on forehead between two eye brows, on throat, on navel, on different glands and points of nervous system and on different points of the body, psychic centres.

He perceived as a major breakthrough. He felt new vigour in his body and mind. He asked his co-monks to undergo the exercise. They felt the change and complimented Muni Nathmal for this.

He laid down a proper procedure comprising breathing techniques, meditation, progressive relaxation practice, and visualization of physical and biological activities inside the body, self analysis and altruism and its impacts on mind and body. He presented his conclusions of thoroughly tested series of exercises put in a *sutra,* thread, to his Guru for public consumption.

Acharya Tulsi was very happy that years' long efforts have been fruitful and the process was named "Prekshya Dhyan", perceptive meditation. "Prekshya Dhyan" consists of the perception of the body, the psychic centres, breath and of contemplation processes which will initiate the process of personal transformation.

Muni Nathmal was a Jain monk. He himself was a self-disciplined monk and quite aware of his limitations and responsibilities. But he was an independent thinker and his thinking and working have originality. Spirituality is a journey of disengaging the knower from the world of physics and engaging the knower in knowing or realizing the self. Perceptive meditation is purely a spiritual process, which takes one to the Self. It is a scientific process. It operates on the basis of cause-effect relationship.

Muni Nathmal demonstrated that spiritual experience could stand on the same footing as scientific truths, being based on experimentation, observation and verification. The inherent power which exists within the Self can be developed and utilized for becoming one's own doctor, psychiatrist, guide and even best friend. Scientific researches have backed up the conviction that preceptive meditation can bring about fundamental and striking changes at physical, mental and emotional levels. It is an internal catharsis approach to keep the body healthy, mind burden free and extend control over emotions so that one can live each day fully by choice and not by default.

Oxygenation of cells is most essential for life as it generates energy for life activities, activates conscious centre and increases our awareness of what is happening inside us – physically, mentally and emotionally. Perceptive meditation makes us completely absorbed in what we are doing and allows us to engage the world more fully and to increase our awareness.

Hundred of people had been trained as trainers under the guidance of Muni Nathmal. These trainers had organized meditation camps all over India and benefited thousands of people. All of them had been extremely benefited in developing their spiritual faculties as well as positive attitudes and thinking and also attained freedom from bad habits due to addiction to intoxicants, emotional imbalance or other nervous or endocrine disorders by bio-chemical and bio-electrical changes in the body through preceptive meditation. Through this technique it has been observed that endocrinal hormones are balanced and emotional intelligence is enriched, negative emotions are overcome, metabolic activities are regulated and stress effectively is managed.

The practice of perceptive meditation has opened a new chapter in philosophical thinking. He continued his research, discourse and debate. "Science of Living" is his effort to make our body, breath, speech and mind truly accomplished or well-trained through the process of *preksha,* seeing or perceiving carefully and profoundly *anupreksha,* contemplation, *Kayosagga,* total relaxation and spiritual vigilance (awakening of the consciousness and its constant alertness) for revival of values and fuller development of human personality.

The WHO reports that over one million people commit suicide every year. This highlights the gross imbalance in material and spiritual values in contemporary society. Increasingly, people live for only worldly goals. Their entire sense of identity and self worth comes from the pursuit and achievement of materialistic aims such as wealth, sensual pleasure, possessions and positions. This definition of success in terms of material achievements lies at the root of suicidal thought.

It is especially among the so-called educated that a large proportion is found to be without moral backbone. In the absence of proper emotional development, such reprehensible activities are only natural because if a person is devoid of tender feelings like love, compassion, tolerance, patience, contentment, altruism, etc. It would therefore not be surprising if such a person then indulges in violence, crime or other unethical activities or even suicide.

In ancient India, education combined knowledge and system of physical, mental and spiritual unfoldment by simple and scientific methods of concentration and meditation.

The modern mode of learning, in particular, is a veritable hotchpotch of incompatibles; it brings about mental indigestion in many instances. Education is confined itself to intellectual development, alone, and has, therefore, failed to fulfil the expectation which society has from it. Its aim should be to build up the human being but despite manifold increase in the number of higher education institutions like colleges, universities etc., the criminal and beastly tendencies of man are increasing.

Imbuing his philosophical quest with the spirit of scientific inquiry Muni Nathmal identified that all attitudes and behaviour of man are intrinsically controlled by the subtle most level of consciousness through various biological processes. One's own effort can bring about a transformation in them. He emphasized that modern education is constantly improving methods of intellectuals but it badly needs to be supplemented with moral and spiritual training.

The care and spiritual nourishment of the early life usually determines its later development and therefore training for this should start from school level.

Muni Nathmal prepared a theme of education for training and harmonizing man's physical, mental and spiritual nature and discussed its relevance in a conclave of teachers, academicians, education ministers of state and central governments.

It was concluded that moral and spiritual values, without whose appreciation no one can approach happiness, cannot be inculcated merely by inclusion in the formal curriculum. Spiritual progress is not possible without practice. No human being can succeed in life without the development of resolute will-power. Strong will-power liberates us from undesirable conduct and guides us towards right conduct.

The exercises of auto suggestion *(bhavana)* coupled with concentration on psychic centres and breath control bring about required internal (chemical and electrical) changes with the ultimate result of transformation of personality.

Mahavira said, "Right conduct is the essence of knowledge". Teachers need to be trained first in this technique of Science of Living. He prepared a course for teachers for their training.

A course of training in Non-violence for all people was devised by Muni Nathmal. It is based on the technique of "Change of Heart" or more precisely, ordering of neuron-endocrine system to purge the human consciousness of all its negative attitudes and instincts that give rise to violence, cruelty, retaliation, greediness, meanness, selfishness etc. by nullifying the effect of deluding *karma* and thus bringing about the desirable change in the autonomous working of neuron-endocrine system.

Value-oriented techniques have been prescribed to inculcate moral and spiritual values. A student is made to study less and more time and energy is devoted to practice and experimentation on the self. The syllabus of Science of Living has been formulated for all levels of students beginning from class-1 up to graduation standard.

The human nature can undoubtedly be changed. The experiments in the field of Science of Living have proved to be blessings for the individual. These experiments have succeeded in bringing about all-round development of body, mind, intellect and emotions. In statistical terms, millions of students, thousands of teachers and hundreds of intellectuals have witnessed the sprouting of the seeds of change in their nature, behaviour and conduct during the last many years. It has won acceptance with many educational bodies like NCERT, NCTE and others.

Muni Nathmal was a versatile writer and a fine orator. His style was simple and captivating. He worked with all forms of literature. His poetry employs deep philosophic truth in emotional appealing terms. His epic, *Sambodhi* represents the soaring heights of his poetic capabilities. The rhythmic conversation between Mahavira and the prince-monk, Megha Kumar, explains the knot of life and philosophy. Another book, *Rishabhayana* gives a glimpse of his maturity as a poet. He has revealed in the art of playwriting in the form of traditional Sanskrit dramas like *Asru Veena* and *Ratnapalacharitam*.

Using the imagery within the language of Sanskrit and weaving the wisdom of nature with man's power that lies beyond the mind he delved freely and easily into the world of fiction. His plays, conscious of stagecraft and of the viewer's involvement takes him or her from the mundane to the sacred with the ease and felicity of an artist.

Emerging from long years of penance, undeterred dedication and deep sincerity in the spiritual path Muni Nathmal was able to study obscure and unfathomable aspect of lifestyle of Mahavira and his spiritual discipline. When he revealed in his book, *Shraman Mahavira,* that he could establish contact with Mahavira, Devadhirgani Chhamashraman and Acharya Kunda Kunda, the great Jain scholar of 2nd century, to know more about the life of Mahavira, it put others in a state of thunder-struck. He empathetically said that all this was possible by the infinite power of the soul.

Acharya Tulsi received many compliments for Muni Nathmal. One popular Hindi poet called Muni Nathmal Vivekananda of day; the others were impressed by Muni Nathmal's mental prowess. Some were impressed by Muni Nathmal's simplicity, the others for his dedication to his Guru. Intelligentsia were his followers and a large numbers were impressed by his mammoth literature. One university offered him D.Lit. and the other institution offered him its highest award. Followers of Acharya Tulsi told him that they were very lucky that they got Acharya like him but he too was more lucky he got a disciple like Muni Nathmal.

Muni Nathmal heard their praise in stoic silence. He accepted the awards with characteristic modesty but did not accept what is material. On October 1978 Acharya Tulsi conferred epithet "Mahaprajna" upon him for his vast knowledge and extraordinary mental and analytical power. This became his new name on February 4, 1979 when Acharya Tulsi declared him *Yuvacharya,* successor-designate and changed his name to Mahaprajna. Muni Nathmal's new name becomes Yuvacharya Mahaprajna. Alas! if Acharya Kalugani were alive to see that Valkalchiri became Mahaprajna, a stage between wisdom and absolute knowledge.

Muni Nathmal remained uninfluenced by all this development. This was the story of Muni Nathmal. Many pleasantries are connected to the name, which seems to have been long lost. An old acquaintance of Nathmal conjectured and found the fugitive, he became humble. There was hardly any taker of the story that he carried with the *buddu* tag before he entered the great sermonising career, while the childhood prediction was vindicated.

The *dharma* in Jainism is preached by the most pure and holy, by those who have been completely free from all attachments, avarice and infatuations seeking to attain *nirvana* or eternal bliss. Authorized Jain *muni* or *acharya* are the prime teachers of Jainism. Their travel is limited only to areas that can be traversed on foot. Therefore, many regions of India as well as abroad have been deprived of the understanding of Jainism and Jainism could not spread and remain confined within a limited territory and did not attain the same international stature as Buddhism because it has tougher rules than Buddhism. Jain monks have to wear a white cloth on their mouths and do not touch most things, including money and electronic items.

In the modern age Veerchand Gandhi was the first Jain who sailed abroad and propounded the philosophy of Jainism. He and Swami Vivekanand went to USA to attend the Parliament of World Religion Conference in 1893. This young man of twenty-nine, impressed the delegates not only by his eloquence, but also by the sheer weight of his scholarship.

He stayed in the USA for about two years after the conference and lectured in cities such as Chicago, Boston, New York, and Washington. He also visited England, France, Germany and other places in Europe. He delivered over five hundred lectures on Jainism, meditation, Indian systems of philosophy, Indian culture, occultism, and spiritualism. His discourses convinced the elite of America of the fact that the Jain religion has an authentic and rational religious tradition.

He was accorded a warm reception and shown highest spiritual associations in the USA and other countries. Though he was only a house-holder and not a monk or religious preacher, he expounded so well. Who must then be his Guru? His simple but striking philosophy of life is worth knowing, worth understanding.

The influence of Vivekanand's philosophy has been kept alive by his disciples by founding organization, like Ramkrishna Mission, whereas no attempt has been made to keep Veerchand Gandhi's memory alive.

Over the years people of Jain faith have travelled to countries outside India in significant numbers. The migration that started as individuals slowly grew with the addition of their families and friends who coalesced into groups and eventually their own society. As a result, practicing Jains felt the need to build an edifice where people could unite and share their knowledge. This eventually led to Jain temples and institutions around the world to worship and perform religious rites and activities together.

The growing networked society is indeed very encouraging for Jains outside India, yet the awareness of Jainism remains limited primarily to Jains. With the growing awareness of vegetarianism, which is a synonym of Jainism, other than Jains are made to know the benefits that Jainism can bring to daily life in all societies. Jainism's stance on non-violence goes far beyond vegetarianism. Jainism is not defined as a religion or sect, but a "practice of living", which may help people in all strata and resolve many of the imbalances in the universe.

Conventions, meditation, yoga camps, spiritual seminars and other religious efforts are the ways through which one can understand the religious values and their importance in modern age. The intention of arranging this kind of activities is to minimize the individual selfishness and develop the feelings of humanity and unity. But only by attending such spiritual events is not enough. To create a peaceful, healthy and balanced environment one has to bridge the gap between knowledge and conduct by practicing Jainism in daily life.

Mahavira made Jainism the focal point for the students of other schools of thoughts as well. Mahavira himself was a *Kshatriya,* warrior class. He knew that the *Brahmins,* scholars of Vedant, of that time were highly learned and could understand, analyze and propagate his doctrines. Accordingly, he made highly learned *Brahmins* his main disciples. Among his followers were not only the people of India but they belonged also to Gandhar, Kapisha and Parsika.

To increase the greater understanding of Jainism, Jain philosophers, scholars and propagators were to be prepared and required to be sent to areas not covered by Jain monks and nuns. Attunement of Yuvacharya Mahaprajna with his Guru was exemplary. What Acharya Tulsi thought was also on the mind of Yuvacharya Mahaprajna.

In 1980 Acharya Tulsi and Yuvacharya Mahaprajna felt the necessity of the hour and took a very bold and progressive step. They created a new category of Jain novices, the *saman order,* intermediate between mendicants and laity for the dual purpose of spreading the Jain doctrine all over the world and to teach the new socio-religious programmes of moral transformation of humankind.

Samans follow the lifestyle of Jain mendicants, but they are granted permissions to use means of transportation and allowed to eat food which is prepared for them, which are traditionally prohibited for fully initiated Jain mendicants.

In 1994 Acharya Tulsi was in his 80th year, 70 years of his monkhood. He was full of enthusiasm, love and spiritual glory. Age was no bar for him. He relinquished the post of Acharya, though he looked well and strong, and conferred the same on Yuvacharya Mahaprajna on 18th February 1994 and consecrated him as the tenth Acharya of Terapanth.

He wanted that he be called *Sant,* an ordinary *muni,* Tulsi. This did not meet the eyes of millions of his followers. They called him *Ganadhipati* Tulsi and Acharya Mahaprajna referred to him as *Gurudeva.* He wished that Acharya Mahaprajna should be more glorious Acharya than him during his life time, of which Sadhvi Baluji had a premonition and declared much earlier in her life time.

Acharya Tulsi left this world on June 23, 1997 and entered into a final ecstasy from which he never returned to ordinary consciousness. This was devastating news for his followers. Acharya Mahaprajna took it as the law of nature and went into deep silence. He handed over body of his *Gurudeva* to conduct solemn rights. He bore his *Gurudeva* in his mind and continued to carry his mission more vigorously. His Guru's omniscient guidance is with him. Since then not a single day has passed that he did not recall his name. This is a story of a great Guru and his great disciple. History repeated itself after two and half millennium and has left its footprints for ever.

Acharya Mahaprajna worked on the same track as that of his Guru. He discovered more avenues of growth. He made vigorous efforts to promote international understanding, goodwill and friendship through a variety of constructive programmes which included organization of international conferences with varying themes, propagation of Anuvrat Movement which enjoined individuals to pledge themselves to strengthen ties of friendship among the peoples of the world irrespective of nationality, religion, caste and colour, creation of awareness among people by organizing non-violence training camps on a large scale.

In 1998, World Rights, Norway, organized international peace conference in the presence of Acharya Mahaprajna. The representatives from Noble Peace Institute, UNESCO, Peace Research Institute, Oslo, and other international peace organizations attended along with prominent personalities from India. This conference, aimed at uniting various forces striving for world peace and non-violence as well as drawing a commonly acceptable plan to eradicate the violent factors from the face of this world, would prove to be a fruitful step in the direction of creating an atmosphere congenial for the new world order based on permanent peace, amity, and spiritual bliss.

The Anuvrat Vishva Bharati, which is the institute established for promotion of Anuvrat in the international field, has so far organized three successful International Conferences on Peace and found warm response from important International Organisations like UNO, UNESCO, UN University for Peace (Costa Rica) and many other NGO's.

An International Dialogue on "Non-Violence Training and Education" was successfully organized in 1995 at university campus of Ladnun, in which besides Acharya Mahaprajna, several international authorities on the subject had participated. Prof. Glenn D. Paige from Hawaii University, Prof. Johan Galtung from France, Mr. Bernard Lafayette, Jr. from U.S.A., Mr. Charles Alphin from U.S.A., and Ms. Robin Ludwig from UNO had a two day long discussion on the topic which ended in producing a very important document in the field of peace activity.

Acharya Mahaprajna was a great philosopher and thinker with an intuitive insight, his speeches made such deep impression on the audience that whatever he suggested was easily accepted by people. Only because of his great acumen, is the rationale of the need of peace through non-violence brought home.

Acharya Mahaprajna embarked on a four-year *Ahimsa Yatra,* peace march, through Rajasthan, Gujarat, Maharashtra, and Madhya Pradesh, in December 2001. "Something needed to be done about *Ahimsa,* which is not about no wars and no killings. Even domestic violence and anger are forms of violence," he explained. The peace march marked the 2600th birth anniversary of Mahavira.

Civilization has become confused with multiplicity of material possession and the fever-chart of an ever rising standard of comfort. The objective of modern economics is prosperity. It aims at everyone becoming rich. In order to fulfil the objective of pervasive prosperity, it also expects that desires, needs and production are expanded, and as a consequence thereof, greed promoted. The expanding greed presupposes expanded needs, which calls for expanding production for higher economic growth. Economic growth calls for competition. In this context, peace and non-violence are relegated to a secondary position.

In ancient times religion and politics were interlinked. Today, money is the pivot around which society moves. People no longer give religion and faith the same priority. Post-industrial revolution, developed nations acquired dominant control over world resources. Powerful nations became more of a threat than source of strength, as they had their eyes on economic empire-building. A new type of imperialism, exercise of power through economic control, rather than through direct political control, has emerged. In the name of patriotism and national progress, and on the plea of establishing peace and spreading civilisation, are bringing about utter ruin to the weak and backward nations by robbing them of their wealth and possession.

As industries become centralized, it will lead to exploitation and exploitation through power and violence. Exploitation is not be limited to one country but it is extended to exploitation of one nation by another.

The nations with increased industrial capacity use that power to exploit other nations. Where industrialisation gets a free hand, the problem of conflict and war is also created and industrial pollution began to threaten the environment.

Mahavira said that the one, who rejects the people and the world, rejects his own existence; and the one who rejects his own existence rejects the existence of the world. He said: "Do not reject the existence of the world and do not reject your existence as well. The most important principle of environment is that you are not the only element. When you do something for yourself you must know that your action/s will impact the entire world." So what can an individual do? How do his actions affect the rest of the world?

Mahavira too maintained that where self-restraint and peace prevail, non-violence is also ensured. Satisfaction and enjoyment have remained the main targets of economics. To Mahavira, the peace was the highest treasure, where wealth was secondary. When the objective of peace becomes primary, the whole approach changes. When peace is primary, the purity of means gains supremacy.

Jainism teaches practicing prudency and curbing of wants, while, at first look economics seems to be going exactly opposite. Economics and religion apparently seem to be aliens and there have been several attempts to bring forth convergence between the two.

Acharya Mahaprajna wrote a book, *Economics of Mahavira,* wherein he tries to propound a new concept of economics of non-violence to make people aware of person-centred non-violence and society-centred non-violence to give more importance to cooperation rather than competition; to sustainability rather than destruction, to co-existence rather than independent existence; to restraints rather than increase in human desires and wants, to respect for different views rather than pursuit of absolutist views and thus leads to a more harmonious and greater peaceful existence for all nations.

In fact, in the world of economics itself, there is a vigorous new thrust being given to economics of non-exploitation, which seems to be coming extremely close to Acharya Mahaprajna's notion of economics of non-violence and path of convergence. With a view to exchanging views on the above model of economics and the concept that economic growth remains rooted in peace and that more and more people join hands together to carry the message beyond the national frontier an international conference was organized in Delhi in December 2005. The delegates unanimously endorsed the model of non-violence-oriented system.

Acharya Mahaprajna held regular inter-faith talks and organized peace seminars where representatives from various religions were invited to discuss social and moral problems of the world.

□

IV

VARDHMANA, Prosperous One, – with his conception in the family, the family had increased in wealth, in power, in prosperity – was born in a princely family. He was surrounded by all the luxuries and pleasure the world had to offer. He simply realized that there is more to life than the endless pursuit of fame, fortune and power. In fact, fame, fortune and power are merely means to the end. They create fear and curtail freedom. This notion was not based on any intellectual or philosophical theories; rather it was based on his own experience.

Vardhmana inherited from his parents not only the latent impressions of democratic thought, but grew in the open minded environment of the oligarchic republic, whose government was vested in a senate, composed of the elected resident members and presided over by an officer who had the title of the king. The king used to get this office by election. His election was for a specific term.

King chaired the senate. Decisions of the senate dictated his governance. In the senate, the rule of quorum was applied. The proposal was read thrice, and then it went through the democratic process of discussion, debate and voting. The vote was kept secret. Meetings were held in the council hall. The members had to maintain decorum. There was provision for bringing a motion of condemnation against a member for despicable behaviour.

Many republics when combined made a confederacy. The status and rights of all the members of the confederacy were equal. The *Vajjis* to whom the *Jnatris* belonged were a large confederacy, which had within its fold at least eight clans the *Videhas,* the *Licchavis,* the *Jnatris* etc. The *Vajji* confederacy was the foremost and powerful. Its capital was Vaishali and its contemporaries were under the sway of its power. The powerful monarchy of Magadh also thought it better to seek friendly relations with its members.

Thus, Vardhmana witnessed freedom for all, equality of everyone, autonomy, negation of a dynasty system, freedom of expression, discussion and debate, complete transparency in the decision-making process, non-interference, mutual respect for regional rights, the spirit of co-existence and the benefits of good human behaviour not only within the gambit of a limited focus of republic but within the wider arena of larger confederacy to the *Vajji* confederacy. Besides the strong and highly developed legacy of thought right from the first Tirthankar Adinath to the twenty-third Tirthankar Parshvanath, the scenario of goodness of the contemporary age may have naturally influenced Vardhmana.

On November 30, 570 B.C. at the age of 30, with the consent of his immediate family Vardhmana left the palace in pursuit of knowledge of ultimate nature of being and the world. He gave up every thing, including his ornaments and clothes and renounced the sensual world.

He pulled off his hair by his hands and initiated himself as a Jain monk, a life of mendicancy and self-denial. He started touring various parts of the country.

He all alone naked and silent plunged into the jungle full of beasts of all kinds, where vines and creepers grew about him as he remained oblivious to food, people and elements. He lived in rains as also burning sun under trees. He never wore any covering whatsoever. He lived in barbarians and savage tribes. He was struck with stick, or with fist or with lance-head or with slaps or with earth-cold or with potsherd. They would cry with joy while striking him once and again. Some people, throwing him up, made him fall down, or they pushed him out of his seat. Abandoning his body, and completely dedicated to the soul, he endured all sorts of mistreatments with great fortitude, without any pre-made resolve.

He chose the path full of thorns and pebbles. He lived in dreary and dilapidated buildings rumoured to be haunted by demons and ghosts. Fear never touched him. Like an armoured hero at the head of the battle, Mahavira was armoured with self-restraint. He tolerated all hardships, remaining unmoved from meditation and continued his travels.

He conquered sleeping, the senses and the hardships. He attained ultimate happiness by overcoming craving in all forms. He did away entirely with the consciousness of matter. He shut off all five senses and sensations pouring in through the sensory nerves striving to realise Himself and realise the nothing of all things but the Self.

He conquered inner enemies such as ego, pride, anger and delusion. The struggles of the battlefields pale into insignificance when man contends with internal enemies. He became Mahavira, all conquerors. He was fearless and therefore truly free – real freedom when soul is free from all *karmic* matters.

Fearlessness is real freedom. Non-violence was the natural corollary of his teaching of fearlessness. Only the one who has transcended fear can experience equanimity, essential to a correct understanding of the human situation in the world.

After twelve and half long years of austerity and self-purification he crossed all hurdles of the path of meditation. There was no thought, no object, no dream, no desire, nothing – just emptiness in his mind. His mind was thought-free. It was perfect silence. His consciousness became pure. The inner world of soul opened up. His inner quietness, inner silence, was filled with inner light. He was knower, all aware, fully inside. He was independent and thus self-contained and self-assured.

He knew his own being and that being all pervading. Knowing oneself means knowing all. He got the knowledge of all reality. With this enhanced vision he could glance and gaze past, present and future and got satisfactory solutions for all those problems and questions connected with the life and the universe which occur to any inquisitive soul.

He investigated reality through uncompromising self-control and contemplation, unruffled by the passing events of the transitory life. Truth emerged through intuitive thoughts and true vision from his experience, penance and empirical evidence. His vision widened. Now Mahavira was enlightened.

He standardized and codified natural behaviour of entities and visualize the truth of *Ahimsa, Aparigrah, Anekant* and *Syadvad,* and underline the need for catholicity, endurance and respect for others in human behaviour.

Mahavira said, "Everything natural is living and his message reflects freedom and spiritual joy of the living beings. All living beings, irrespective of their size, shape, and form how spiritually developed or undeveloped, are equal and we should love and respect them. Nothing which breathes, which exists, which lives, or which has essence or potential of life, should be destroyed or ruled over, or subjugated, or harmed, or denied of its essence or potential."

Human beings as one of the numerous species, have no extra rights than any other species. They wish to live as much as we do; they have feelings and emotions. They have love and passion; they fear death as much as we do. Their instinct for life is no less than ours. Their right to live is as fundamental as our own.

Mahavira taught the idea of supremacy of human life and stressed the importance of the positive attitude of life. The human soul can be saved from *karmic* blemish by practicing severe asceticism and austere life can be made possible through non-violence towards all living creatures.

Only human life enables us to search for knowledge and understand our spiritual nature. Not only do humans have no absolute rights — to take, to control, or to subjugate other forms of life — but they also have extra obligations to practise non-violence, i.e., to give protection, be kind and caring towards all living beings, and to be tolerant towards all creation's life-styles and ideologies.

Violence arising out of day to day activities, i.e., occupational violence and violence arising out of self defence may be justifiable, but nevertheless they are violence. It is difficult to avoid this type of violence completely, but one must try and minimise it. Even such violence must only be indulged in when we are absolutely compelled to do so. Not out of anger, attachment, pride or ego.

Violence may be of any type, its sin and the level is decided by the person's intent or mental attitude, which matters more than the act. Where both mental and physical violence occur, that is the cause of more sin, more bondage. Intentional, deliberate violence is neither important for life nor for the country or family. We indulge in intentional violence only to appease our ego or out of attachment. This type of violence destroys the soul. Such an act is bounded by *Karma* and is a sin.

Non-violence is not just in act but also at the level of thoughts and speech. It consists of not even desiring to do wrong. Violence may be committed, commissioned or consented to. Mahavira said that non-violence must begin in the mind. Unless the mind is compassionate, non-violence is not possible. Unless one is at ease in the inner world, one cannot practice non-violence in the external world. If the mind is condemning other people yet the tongue speaks sweet words, then that is not non-violence. The seeds of non-violence live within the inner consciousness.

Keeping consciousness pure is therefore, an essential part of non-violence. Pure consciousness means consciousness that is uncorrupted, uncontaminated and undiluted with the desire to control others.

Non-violence of the mind should be translated into non-violence of speech. Harmful, harsh, untrue, unnecessary, unpleasant and offensive speech is violence. Skilful use of language is a sacred skill. Mahavira insisted that we must understand others fully before we speak. Language can express only partial truth; therefore, non-violence is an essential guide to our spoken words.

Non-violence of mind and speech leads to the non-violence of action. Ends cannot justify means. Means must be compatible with ends. Therefore, all human actions must be friendly, compassionate and unaggressive. Non-violence should be practised in all its aspects and we should abstain from committing injury in nine possible ways. We should not commit through mind, speech and body and each through the manner of personally committed, commissioned through others and giving consent for commitment by others. He suggested four means — truth, non-stealing, chastity and non-possessiveness — to purify the mind. It is a kind of soul exercise to keep the inner world healthy and pure.

Truth means understanding and realizing the true nature of existence and the true nature of oneself; accepting reality as it is and being truthful to it, seeing things as they are without judging them as good or bad. It means "Do not lie" in its deepest sense: do not have illusions about yourself. Face the truth without fear. Things are as they are. A person of truth goes beyond mental constructs and realizes existence as it is. A wise ascetic should speak exactly what he has seen; his speech should be brief, free from ambiguity and clearly expressed. His speech should neither be deceptive nor cause anxiety to anyone.

Living in truth means that we avoid manipulating people or nature because there is no one single truth that any mind can grasp or tongue can express. Being truthful involves being humble and open to new discoveries, and yet accepting that there is no final or ultimate discovery.

Truthfulness is asceticism of speech. Truth is what it is: we accept what is as it is, speaking of it as it is, and lives it as it is. Any individual or group claiming to know the whole truth is by definition engaged in falsehood. Ultimately, existence is a great mystery.

Non-stealing means refraining from acquiring goods or services beyond one's essential needs. It is difficult to know what the essential needs are, so we should assess, examine and question, day by day, what our need is and what is our greed. The distinction between need and greed can be blurred and therefore the examination of need should be carried out with honesty.

"Do not steal" goes further than any legal definition. If we take more from nature to meets our essential need, we are stealing from nature. For example, clearing an entire forest would be seen as a violation of nature's rights and as theft. Similarly, taking from society in the form of housing, food and clothing in excess of one's essential requirements means depriving other people and is therefore theft. If we are using up finite resources at a greater speed than they can be replenished, then we are stealing from future generations.

Attraction for other's property, attachment, desire, non-restraint, greed, malpractices in trade and taking other's articles without permission—all these amount to stealing. We should give first and then take. Taking before giving is 'stealing'.

Chastity is love without lust or restraint of senses, which means renunciation of lustful desire. A living body is not merely an integration of limbs and flesh but it is the abode of the soul which potentially has perfect perception, perfect knowledge, perfect power and perfect bliss. It should not only be kept in perfect order by careful actions of mind and body but any thoughts, speech, or acts that demean, debase, or abuse the body are against the principle of chastity.

Chastity has been classified as a great virtue, a great charm of all values. Chastity has implication beyond sexual temperance. The fullest development of body, mind and intelligence is not possible without control of the sexual instinct.

Celibacy has an extensive creative power because it is the most effective means of developing and liberating the inner consciousness. Its observation without a break develops *Medha*, the nerve of retentive faculty and intuition. From this arises the capacity for grasping and retaining power. And unless lust is controlled and strict chastity is observed, the mind never becomes quiet, perfect meditation and concentration are not possible.

For spiritual road one has to remain absolutely pure. One can train one's inner powers only if one is completely contented. For monks, it means total abstinence from sensual pleasure, and for lay people it means fidelity in marriage.

Non-possessiveness means no accumulation of material

things; sharing and living without ostentation and without a display of wealth, dress, food and furnishings. Less we spend too much time in the care of possessions more time we will have for the care of the soul.

It is on account of attachment that a person commits violence, utters lies, commits theft, indulges in sex and develops a yearning for unlimited hoardings.

We should not acquire what is not necessary, recognizing that whatever you acquire will bind you tightly. Free you from non-essential acquisitions and you will gain real freedom.

Mahavira taught a scientific explanation of nature, meaning of life and a guide as to how we should behave to draw this real nature and meaning into our own life. He taught that one should lead a life of 'simplicity': 'self-restraint', 'sufficiency' and 'frugality'. Being satisfied with less is self-control. The idea that whatever we have, or however much we have, is never enough is the source of anguish. One should move from "more and more" to "enough"! There is nothing lacking in the world.

There is the abundance of Nature. Only when we want to own, control and possess it, we create scarcity. Because we can never possess everything, we always want more. This possessiveness is the source of scarcity.

The moment we are satisfied, and don't want to control and possess, we have abundance. Paradoxically this abundance is only available to those who can learn to live within the limits of one's needs. Enjoyment without renunciation is all suffering. It broadens the heart and cheers the mind.

Mahavira said that the mind is that fierce, unruly and

dreadful horse which runs hither and thither in all directions. It should be controlled by the discipline of *Dharma* so that it becomes a well-trained steed. Just as a monkey cannot sit still even for a single moment, so also the mind cannot remain free from evil thoughts even for a single moment. The consciousness gets contaminated by ego, greed, pride, anger and fear. Souls suffer because of desires, attachments and anguish. Mahavira devised ways to purify the mind, the soul and the consciousness.

He recognized the partial and incomplete nature of ordinary human knowledge. Desire, hatred, pride, anger and greed stem from partial one-sided understanding of things dogmatically presumed to be the whole truth. How many times have we embarrassingly realized the inappropriateness of our anger, jealousy, pride, or greed when we came to see the "full picture"? Greed for money vanishes when it is understood that money can't buy health, friends or happiness.

Excessive pride gives way to humility when we come to appreciate the wonderful qualities and accomplishments of others. Anger and hatred disappear when we realize that other objects, situations, or persons are no threat to us. To the extent that we appreciate that the knowledge from which the destructive passion arise is partial, we are encouraged to restrain ourselves until our understanding increases.

Mahavira laid great stress on mutual understanding, tolerance and understanding the viewpoint of others. He did not accept a one-sided view in any field—from this point of view, his doctrine of *Anekatavad*, non-absolutism, i.e., Theory of Mani-foldness of Reality, a method that allows for reconciliation, integration and synthesis of conflicting views, is invaluable.

Jain scriptures say that there is no universal truth but a subjective truth which differed from one person to the other. Knowledge is accessible according to an individual's means. Each individual is in possession of his own knowledge which is confined to him. There is no strict rule that governs knowledge. It is totally individual and subjective. Absolute negation or absolute affirmation is impossible in the case of knowledge in the sense that the individual could both believe and disbelieve in any theory of knowledge. The theory of *syadvada,* seven-fold formula, or the concept of reality which is indeterminate, forms the basis for *anekatavad. Syadvada* stems from the word *syat* which means may be. *Syadvad a* indicated that an argument can be examined from many points of view.

Mahavira emphasized the need of a comprehensive outlook. He said, "Modes and laws are infinite." The "Real" means that which is existent at a particular time. One cannot lay claim to total knowledge just by knowing a few laws. It is indispensable to acquire full knowledge of Truth. Truth perceived from different angles appears contradictory, but in reality these partial visions are complimentary.

Matter may be small or large, living or non-living, it is so vast that we cannot realise it in its entirety at the same time. Every substance in the universe is related to every other substance. Thus reality is manifold. Due to relativity, matter has many attributes. The truth about any object or substance consists in the recognition that it contains various properties from various standpoints and that its characterisation in terms of some of them does not exclude or contradict its characterisation in terms of others. *Anekant* establishes the truth not by rejecting the partial views about reality but by taking all of them into consideration.

Mahavira's *Anekant* doctrine lays strong emphasis on *Samyaktava,* rationality and logic. The ultimate principle should always be logical and no principle can be devoid of logic or reason. The complex and multifaceted nature of reality should be examined from a relative point of view of time, space, substance, mode. To ignore the complexity of reality is to commit the fallacy of dogmatism. It is the logic that guarantees our capacity to know and provides us with criteria by which we should be able to test our knowledge.

Anekant means non-insistence on one's viewpoint only. It accommodates to listen and regard the views of others as well. It discards absolutism of thought, mental reservations, and misunderstanding. It propounds mutual understanding.

The doctrine of *Anekant* reinforced intellectual and philosophical foundation of relativism and adopts the policy of co-existence. It is a complete guide to the practical life. *Anekant* logic helps us to understand others' points of view. This way clashes would have been banished and an era of global peace would have prevailed.

Mahavira is not merely an apotheosis or a deified ideal. He has shown us by the examples of his own life experiences that non-violence and compassion are the answers for peace and well being. In order to expunge violence, one has to remove it from thoughts, from feelings, from the mind, and from one's expression. Knowing this law of life, we can purify our minds with meditation and understanding.

Mahavira said, "Practice thyself and show the path to others". Acharya Mahaprajna not only set an admirable example of living the ideals of non-violence devoutly but also spreading his message widely. He had a large cohort of saints and nuns numbering over a thousand which included, a Yuvacharya, Chief of Nuns, monks, nuns, saman, samanis, upasaks, who are motivating the countless ignorants on the track of non-violence in every day life by travelling door to door for moral awakening, giving lucid discourses on various national and international issues confronting the world today, encouraging the abandonment of all intoxicants, besides holding conferences, seminars and increasing the consciousness of reverence for all life.

Training in non-violence and establishing a Non-violence Commission is the result of his revolutionary thinking which does not only just theoretical but has practical aspect also.

□

V

MAHAVIRA'S teachings, if faithfully followed, have two results. Firstly, they produce a better society for every creature to live in, and secondly, they enable the individual to improve his/her own inner feelings and character.

The life and philosophy of Mahavira are the unique contribution not only for the Jains but for the mankind as a whole. Mahavira was concerned not only with human rights or rights of being but those of all living and non-living beings. This path of Mahavira is difficult, but once is fully comprehended and put into practice, it is uniquely very simple.

Mahavira did not say to follow what he said or follow the Jain religion. Mahavira said that the realistic religion is consisted of four parts:

1. equality of all living beings,
2. every living soul has right to put self-effort to improve itself and do not take away this right,
3. do not rule other living ones,
4. all views should be viewed with equanimity — without like or dislike.

If only one of these is adopted, other three will automatically be adopted.

Acharya Mahaprajna was a religious teacher. Hell fire or

promise of paradise were not his subject. He has redefined the purpose of religion and connected religion closely to life and taught a religion of simple and rational living.

He was a perfect *yogi* and did not perform any miracle or work wonders, but only discharged his responsibilities without personal motive or attachment, and trod the sure path of enlightenment. He was a spiritually advanced person and the best experimentalist in the history of spirituality with very clear intention and definite goals.

He was a self-taught philosopher and social reformer. To him philosophy is a science of seeing, direct perception of reality and not merely a reasoning based on logical consistency. Lacking a formal education, Acharya Mahaprajna's philosophy was shaped by an amazingly retentive memory and a passion for reading and learning. He was a philosopher of religion and its relation to the human conditions. Consistent with his religion, he often used the teachings of Mahavira and non-violence as the principles and moral expression of his philosophy.

He saw the non-violence as the only solution to the problems of today and wrote many books explaining its role in creating a peaceful society. He also unfurled the idea of non-violence in many aspects: as the other names for diplomacy, as respect for fellow beings and so on.

His writings presented his thoughts on theology, natural laws and man's relation with nature and non-violence. One of his ideals was his embrace of science as tools to spirituality.

He said that our times demanded that everyone entering a religious order need not become exclusively "religious". He must have a scientific outlook. He spurned all misconceptions, sanctimonious rituals and superstition spreads about religion.

Modern man seeks logical solutions. What are the divine truth and how one could find it? In a pluralistic, multi-religious society these questions become more pertinent because each of the institutional religions and their sects give different, and many a time conflicting interpretations of the divine truth. Acharya Mahaprajna was of view that we carry a lot of burden of myths, customs, superstitions and traditions. The deeper meaning of myths or symbol, the religious and historical rationale of a custom or rite be probed or reviewed. Customs and conventions limit our outlook considerably. Once we are out of our prejudices and habits, we can see truly what is right and wrong in any other nationality.

He said, "The religion which does not bring about a change in man's life, which does not impart peace to him, deserves to be discarded rather than carried on as a burden on one's shoulders. Rituals or idol worship alone are not enough unless one's conduct also gets transformed. Unless one is righteous and honest, both to himself and to others, and leads a value oriented life, he is not religious despite his proclamation".

He said that man needs a religion free of all rituals. It is not a process and nor confined to the place of worship. He should live with it all the time. A religion for the contemporary world must be a true guide to daily living, as well as consistent with science.

On the basis of his understanding of the different religions and beliefs Acharya Mahaprajna felt that every religion is beautiful; religion is soul, no matter whether one takes part in Christian communion or make a pilgrimage to Mecca. Religion presents an aspect of truth and collection of all these truths is the ethical basis of human relations and path to progress. The difference amongst religions concerns only the myths and superstitions. The points of agreement among all religions include speaking truth, acquiring knowledge, associating with the good people, controlling sensual passions, cultivating active habits and being honest in dealing with others. Both science and spirituality are quests for truth and so they must work together to get there and bring benefits to mankind.

Acharya Mahaprajna further crystallized this thought through his writings in which both spirituality and science have been projected as mutually complementary. His stand that far from destroying religion science has in fact rejuvenated it is an entirely new concept in religion.

The lesson of life-science of Acharya Mahaprajna has started a movement. Religion believes in sermons whereas science in experimentation. There are so many preachers of religion and so many tenets but still man has not changed.

The life of Acharya Mahaprajna has been unswerving in its pursuit of learning as it was not only from the texts and wisdom of yore but also from every being he interacted with on his experience and insight found expression in his writing both prose and poetry in the form of over 200 books on religion, Jainism, non-violence, history, psychology and personal development, health and spiritual development, colour therapy, mantra and mantra therapy, science and education, truly a vast treasure of wondrous wisdom and instead of getting entangled with problems, he looks for their solution. Perceptive meditation, to awake the self and Science of Living, a value-oriented education programme, are two of his individual contributions to spirituality and education. His enrichment of Indian cultural heritage, especially the incisive analysis of non-violence, has earned him universal acclaim. Those who know him intimately are aware that he was the creator of new perceptions. He was the blending artist of heart and wisdom on one hand and thought and action, on the other.

Acharya Mahaprajna's appeal to the political heads was that for progress peace is the first requirement. Poverty and illiteracy are the sole causes of terrorism and communal disturbance and national wealth should be spent in creating opportunities to every countryman. This will promote equity, the basis of democracy.

The tall slender saint radiated physical, mental and spiritual health. His soft eyes shined with intelligence, sincerity and discrimination. He, a great observer of patience and humility, was meekness personified and was never seen to have lost his temper.

Eight decades of public service, wandering village to village barefoot and lastly in man-driven buggy, wresting daily with practical details and harsh realities, increased his balance, open mindedness, sanity and appreciation of the quaint human spectacle.

He ate only simple food without or with little spices and did not eat fried food. He observed silence once in a fortnight. His balanced life is a source of inspiration that liberation is dependent on inner, rather than outer, renunciation.

On Sunday, May 9, 2010 afternoon at 2.55 pm he left this world and his mortal body merged with the five elements of nature but he will ever remain alive in the memory of the people for his efforts for peace, harmony and well being of humanity.

He was an ideal sage and seer and his writings, actions and philosophy will continue to radiate hope to society.

Soul is my God.
Renunciation is my prayer.
Amity is my devotion.
Self restraint is my strength.
Non-violence is my religion.

ACHARYA MAHAPRAJNA